COUNTER POINT

The Changing Employment Service

Miriam Johnson

**Afterword by
Garth Mangum**

Olympus Publishing Company ⊙ Salt Lake City, Utah

CONTENTS

PREFACE

My first task is to dispel any notion that this book was written by an "evaluator" of the employment service or by an "objective observer." It was not. I was there. I was a participant and a partisan. I worked each station and point, just as they are described here. I either initiated, participated in, or watched most of the developments recounted in these pages. That, of course, determined the choice of material.

It is important that the reader understand this distinction, for just as in the Japanese film "Rashomon," reality may be interpreted differently by each of the participants in the event. There is little doubt that others would view the scenes presented here differently than did I. For example, the agency administrator would undoubtedly select a different set of incidents to illustrate the "turning points" of the organization; he would interpret developments differently. The legislator would explain events in terms of the political implications regarding existing or proposed legislation. And the economist would be inclined to look at the effects of the economy upon the institution.

These points of view are not the concern of this book. Nor is there any attempt at historical comprehensiveness. Instead, the work is based on the premise that there is value to be gained from the participant view. There is value which should be helpful to the agency administrator, the legislator, the economist, and the historian. By focusing on the day-to-day operations at the critical point of contact between agency and client, it should be possible to add a new dimension to the perspective of each observer.

It is my hope that this book will contribute to the climate of intellectual discussion in the manpower field. If it succeeds in moving discussion forward a single small step, it will have served a valid purpose. Productive discussions often begin with questions, and therefore this work is mainly concerned with raising questions rather than answering them. Perhaps there *are* no answers to some of the questions raised in these pages. And that, too, may be an important realization; for in my opinion, there have been too many "certainties" in the past, too many blueprints . . . and too few questions.

Many of the questions which motivated me to write the book were asked by my colleagues in the employment service. I am grateful to them; their thinking entered into and welded with my own. I picked their brains, and I trust they have done the same with me as we shared thoughts in the marketplace of ideas. Their names are too numerous to mention, but I gratefully acknowledge their value to me over many years.

There are, however, three individuals whose contributions to the book must receive specific mention. James Neto, the manpower analyst who heads the Northern California Employment Data and Research section, filled in the gaps of my understanding about the problems relating to labor market information. If those gaps are still apparent in some instances, it is only because I was a poor pupil.

Dorothy Rodighiero worked patiently with me while trying to teach me the difference between a bureaucratic report and a book. If this work still resembles the former on occasion, it is only because old habits die hard. (I can still hear Dorothy saying: "In Heaven's name, never *two* cliches in one sentence.")

Finally, my son, Eric Johnson, lent his incisive mind and his poet's eye to the material, forcing me to think through all the implications of what I was writing and helping me to clarify my thoughts. If the thinking still appears fuzzy in spots, it is because it is not easy for the old to learn all they should from the young.

EMPLOYMENT SERVICE:
Why the Counter Point

Between the conceptualization of a public service and its final implementation lies a tortuous and often devious path. It begins with what the courts call the "intent" of the enabling legislation, winds through the verbiage of the mandate issued by agency policymakers, drifts down through the hierarchy of various administrative levels, and finally reaches the front lines — that point at which service is delivered to the public. The process is the same, whether the initial intent is to provide education, to administer welfare, to ensure civil rights, or to deal with public offenders: A government bureaucracy with responsibility for the particular function must devise a delivery system, presumably to provide a means for the program to find and serve its intended target group.

The consequences of this process are manifold. Often policies enunciated by high level agency spokesmen are altered, diluted, rigidified, or reinterpreted as they move toward the point of implementation. Thus the service finally delivered at the lowest point of the structure may bear little resemblance to the ideals stated in public pronouncements of policymakers and administrators. And the alterations may well be cumulative so that over an extended period of time wide gaps develop between what legislators, administrators, academicians, and the general public assume happens and what actually occurs.

These distortive effects take place within many different contextual frameworks. For example, policy makers sometimes presuppose that a delivery system contains within it a degree of competency and potency which, in fact, proves to be elusive; yet, they predicate entire programs on those elusive competencies. Within another framework, it sometimes happens that the mandate to correct a social ill is charged to the wrong agency because the social ill has been misdiagnosed. And it is not beyond the realm of possibility that an original intent is somehow reversed when attempts are made to act upon it. Finally, an agency may be charged with the task of solving problems which are simply insoluble unless profound changes occur outside the realm of influence of that particular agency or system.

Manpower programs are little different from other social programs in this regard. No matter what the original intent, no matter how tortuous the path from conception to implementation, it is in the local offices of the public employment service throughout the country that most manpower services finally cross over to the recipient. It is at that point where interviewer meets job seeker and programs become reality.

From its inception in 1933 under the Wagner-Peyser Act, the public employment service and its vast network of local offices has been subject to repeated shifts in what it was expected to accomplish. These changing roles have taken shape, have succeeded, or have failed in the local office, right at the edge of the bureaucratic counter where the cumbersome weight of the process falls finally on the shoulders of the single encounter between interviewer and job seeker. The past decade has seen some particularly jarring shifts in the nation's manpower delivery systems. Indeed, the concept of mission has completed a full cycle, and even now the public employment service is grappling with major policy shifts. Its resources are being redirected as manpower policy planners debate the role of the agency and its services.

Should the agency focus chiefly on delivering manpower services to the poor, the welfare recipient, the minority group member, the unskilled worker? Or should it return to a simpler mission such as it had in those halcyon days before 1962 when it sought to place the best man on the job?

The 1973 manpower report to the President declares the latter intent. Undoubtedly, this is partially in response to the fact that the employment service nationally has shown a marked decrease in placement activity over the past decade. There has been a widespread tendency to blame the loss of placements on a policy which many regarded as an excessive concern with the needs of the disadvantaged and little heed to the needs of the employers. But now the state agencies are being pressed by the Department of Labor's regional offices to increase the placement count, and the state agencies are, in turn, pressing the local offices to go back to the numbers game. At the same time, manpower training programs are threatened, "employability services" are being downgraded, and innovation is discouraged. Staff and resources are being redirected toward an all-out effort to win favor with employers. When the shift is accomplished, the employment service will have completed a full circle within little more than a decade — from emphasis upon job placement to emphasis upon solving social problems and back to emphasis upon job placement.

Yet, even the new shift in emphasis is full of ambiguities. The employment service appears irreversibly identified with the welfare problem. Welfare and food stamp recipients by the thousands flood employment service offices across the nation because they are required to make an appearance and register for work. Interviewers in the employment service office are inundated with time-consuming, unproductive paper work which appears to have little relevance to solving the problems of the poor. At the other extreme, the employment service suffers from an historic inability to become an effective and respectable job-matching mechanism. This raises the serious question as to whether or not that mission is a feasible one, whether or not the choices posed by the manpower policy debaters really exist. If the wrong questions are being asked, it is inevitable that wrong answers will emerge.

There is an obvious need to look again at the employment service. Perhaps there is a need to look at it from a different angle, from a different viewpoint. While the transitions of the past decade have been occurring, what has happened at the point of contact in the employment office? How does it all appear from the firing line, looking around and then upward from the lowest point of the structure, from the base, so to speak? As the economy, the political climate, and the nation's manpower policies change, what actually happens in the local office between the job seeker and the professional staff? What part does the employer play? Are the changes in policy reflected in the work performed by an interviewer and in the responses experienced by the job seeker?

Such a perspective can best be achieved by going inside the local office and looking at the duties of the interviewer during various periods of policy emphasis. The California employment service has been selected for this inside view because it — the northern California operation in particular — was unique in the degree to which it embraced the national policy directing the efforts of the agency toward the disadvantaged during the 1960s. It not only adopted nationally designed manpower programs with enthusiasm, but it also initiated considerable innovation which, in turn, impacted itself on the national consciousness. The path of the state toward converting the employment service into an agency committed to serving the poor went all the way to the California Legislature. The Human Resources Development Act became the law in California in 1968. It redirected the agency goals and mandated the allocation of 75 per cent of all manpower development training funds and services to the most severely disadvantaged population.

From this setting, three operating offices in San Francisco at three isolated, significant points in time have been selected for observation. The first office described is actually the synthesis of two downtown local offices in the early part of the 1960s. These offices operated in an identical fashion, but they differed in that each had responsibility for a different set of occupations. At that time the employment service across the nation was concerned primarily with matching the job seeker who came into the office with one of the job openings listed by that office. Although the operation was designed to facilitate the "normal" workings of the labor market, it basically accepted the marketplace as it was and assumed no role for altering any of the components. It sought acceptance and recognition from employers, and it did so partly by attempting to attract the most highly desirable and marketable job seekers. All local offices throughout the country followed operating procedures contained in manuals issued by the federal government; they were uniform in their activities and departed minimally from the standard model.

The second point in time is in the middle 1960s. The office observed is a ghetto outreach office in San Francisco which was known as the Adult Opportunity Center. It was established by the California Department of Employment under an experimental grant resulting from the Manpower Development and Training Act, which was by then fully operational. The office reflected changes in the national social picture. The surge of demand by black citizens for full entry into the "system" was at its height. Nationally, the employment service responded by directing state employment agencies to concentrate greater efforts on behalf of the needful unemployed minority population. There was a marked reduction in the traditional concern over "placement count." The office selected for observation was *not* a synthesis of the outreach effort. In fact, it was a unique experiment. Nevertheless, it serves to describe the forward thrust of adaptation which was possible during that historic era. Innovative efforts such as this and others similar to it contributed to important changes in the perception of manpower policy makers throughout the country, but there is little evidence that such front-line exposure to the minority poor significantly affected subsequent legislative and policy decisions.

The third view from inside an employment service office takes place at the beginning of the 1970s. The level of unemployment was alarmingly high, especially among aerospace professionals, and the forward thrust of demand by blacks had been corroded and diverted. Employment service administrators at the national level were publicly expressing a nostalgic yearning for a return to the mission of the single-minded labor exchange. As a public agency, however, the employment service had never been free of congressional and social pressures to fulfill social needs not necessarily in harmony with the labor exchange function. Special efforts for the old, the very young, the handicapped, and the veteran had been a responsibility of the agency from its very inception. It is obvious to most labor market observers that such focus on so-called "hard-to-place" groups is inimical to the "efficient" operation of a labor exchange. The experiences of the 1960s, with emphases on the poor and the minority groups, had revealed this conflict of purpose more harshly than ever before.

In the same time frame — the early 1970s — it is important that one final observation be made. During the decade under consideration, technology and the "state of the art" continued to develop. New modes and methods for serving the job-seeking public were occasionally attempted on an experimental basis. One such experiment took place in the local office of the city of Hayward, a Bay Area community located some thirty miles from San Francisco. A look inside this experimental office offers important dimension to the operating view of employment services, because it represents both the apex and the apparent end of an era.

Of course, none of these employment service offices existed in isolation. They operated within the context of world, national, and local events, and to a large extent, they reflected these events. They were also subject to social pressures, legislative mandates, administrative changes, staffing variations, and statistical analyses which influenced their direction. The external influences have been described in detail in other studies, but it is important to provide short descriptions of the matrices in which the employment service offices operated. These opening descriptions provide the settings for each of the front-line views offered here. They are not meant to be comprehensive, for they, too, are viewed from the special vantage point at the front counter inside the local employment service office.

It is impossible to experience life in an employment service office without reacting to it, without asking questions. These vignettes should give rise to such questions, and in a final section many questions are verbalized, together with some very personal reactions to the events described in these pages. The questions have to do with basic assumptions behind this nation's manpower programs. But more importantly, they have to do with the ultimate delivery of those programs — and the assumptions on which they are based — to the unemployed individuals who walk through employment service office doors. It is at that point that all programs become reality. And it is from that point that social service programs should ultimately be viewed.

That is the "counter" point.

EARLY 1960s:
The Local Office as a Labor Exchange

From the end of World War II until 1962, when Congress passed the Manpower Development and Training Act, the basic objectives of the public employment service were to assist in "maximizing employment, maintaining job continuity, and sustaining purchasing power." The role was conceived as essentially a a passive one, with no attempt to manipulate or change the elements of the marketplace. Agencies operated on the basis of "the six-point program" developed in 1946, which included the following major features:

- *Placement* — To provide an effective placement service in order to facilitate the employment process for veterans, youth, migrant workers, technologically displaced workers, handicapped and older workers, and all persons seeking jobs.

- *Employment Counseling* — To provide an employment counseling service in order to assist job seekers in making valid occupational choices.

- *Services to Special Applicant Groups* — To provide special assistance and counseling to veterans, youths, older workers, and the handicapped, with the goal of placing these workers in satisfactory jobs.

13

- *Management Services* — to assist employers and labor organizations in the use of tools and techniques to assist in reducing labor turnover. This was to include such things as industrial and job analyses and the development of proficiency or aptitude testing to assist in effective selection, assignment, and transfer of workers.
- *Labor Market Information* — To provide current and valid information on the workings of the labor market for the use of government, job seekers, employers, training authorities, and others.
- *Community Participation* — To cooperate with community organizations by participating in activities and programs designed to increase economic opportunity and raise levels of employment.

The six-point program was within the basic framework of the Wagner-Peyser Act, the 1933 legislation which established the public employment service. As a forerunner of the special concern which was to play an important part in the employment service concept, one of the earliest roles assigned to the service by the Social Security Act of 1935 was to administer the "work" test required by unemployment insurance. But for the most part, the service developed with an employer orientation; that is, except for the special groups delineated by the law, it was devoid of a "service to applicant" element. Of course, it was a "service" to a person if he got a job through the employment service, but the *raison d'etre* was to serve the economy, to act as a personnel arm for employers. It was committed to scanning the labor supply and selecting the "best qualified" of the applicants to satisfy the employers' desires, whatever they were. The only prohibitions were to refrain from supplying "scabs" in the case of labor disputes and to refuse a job order for illegal activities. In some states there were formal prohibitions against accepting a job order which was openly discriminatory, but employers and agency staff had little difficulty in "understanding" each other so far as racial requirements were concerned. Throughout the United States minority workers were considered to be "unacceptable." They were the wrong kind of referral to the vast majority of employers. They were acceptable only in the jobs traditionally performed by blacks and other minorities.

During those years, the employment service made every attempt to "legitimize" itself, to attract the most highly desirable and salable applicants. Specialized placement facilities were developed to serve professional, scientific, and technical workers. The emphasis on placement statistics as a basis for budgeting local office staff made the time spent on more difficult applicants onerous, unprofitable, and distasteful. The conflict between the humane social goals of service to needful people and the behavior necessary to compete for the employers' business was the dilemma that still bedevils the agency throughout the country, at least theoretically. But in 1962 the schizophrenia was less visible.

The Myth of the Labor Exchange

There is a tendency among people for memory to soften reality and to imbue it with a rosy, wistful hue. It is the popular wisdom among employment service staff throughout the country that its problems *began* with the increased emphasis on minorities and the disadvantaged in the mid 1960s. Before that, according to the myth, the employment service played a major and successful role as a labor exchange, with full acceptance by employers and "desirable" applicants alike. A glance at the literature of the period serves to dispel such fanciful notions. It is replete with references to the "bad image" of the employment service which was then attributable to the presence of unemployment insurance claimants. Placements were already in difficulty.

In 1958, long before the policy shifted to helping the disadvantaged, Secretary of Labor James P. Mitchell noted in a speech before the Interstate Conference of Employment Security Agencies that there had been a steady decline in the activities of the employment service and that if it continued the service would affect so small a portion of the nation's workers that it would become questionable whether the expense of maintaining it would be worthwhile.

National placement statistics for the period between 1952 and 1962 reveal that nonagricultural placements (excluding short-time and domestic) dropped from 3.6 million to 3.3 million — a decline of 11 percent — during a period when employees in non-agricultural establishments increased by 13 percent.

Finally, a labor department evaluation of the system completed in August 1958 described the employment service as having been through "eleven years of stalemate, if not progressive decline." The report concluded that the system had access to only a small segment of the labor market and that it was placing fewer people in jobs in 1958 than it had in 1947, despite a national increase of ₄1 percent in nonagricultural employment during the same period.

It is important to put that period, which was free of emphasis on the disadvantaged, into some sort of perspective. For a whole decade (1952-62) there was a total emphasis on placements, on "legitimacy," on winning and retaining the good will of the employer through providing him with the "best qualified," tested, screened, and selected applicants. Few, if any, dichotomous goals were enunciated or emphasized. There was little focus on "service to applicants" or what has come to be regarded by opponents as "hand holding." Disadvantaged and minority job seekers were generally given poorer service or were frozen into occupations and jobs in which there was a traditional demand, not so much because of conscious discrimination as because the system ensured this practice. If, despite these conditions, the employment service was declining in placement effectiveness, it should have raised some very serious questions.

The important question for subsequent decision making was (and still is) why the placement spiral was downward *before* the minority orientation of the 1960s.

There is little doubt that much of the current concern over the employment service is based on a devastating picture provided by the statistics of the past decade. In every area, by every measure, the manpower programs swelled the size of employment service staffs while the measurable activities in terms of placements and new applications plummeted downward. And yet, administrators and policy makers continue to assume that they can increase placements and make significant changes through mere administrative fiat.

The Setting in California and San Francisco circa 1962

In 1962 the California State Employment Service was divided administratively into four areas: Southern California, Los Angeles, interior, and coastal. The last named area covered the geographical area and the administrative structure which will be described in this book. Each area was headed by an area manager. Area offices were responsible for administering three major programs: unemployment insurance, the farm labor service, and the employment service. For purposes of this study, only the last is relevant.

The area line control was maintained through five field supervisors. These individuals supervised approximately 25 local offices in the various communities of the area. In addition to these individuals the area staff included program specialists, a training coordinator, a fairly large staff in the research and statistical section, and the veterans employment representative. The area clearance office dealt with inter- and intrastate job clearances. So-called applicant services were handled by a part-time minority specialist, a part-time handicap specialist, a youth specialist, and an older worker specialist.

In San Francisco two major downtown employment offices were maintained. One handled professional, sales, and commercial occupations; the other covered industrial, service, domestic, and garment occupations. The latter office had previously been divided into industrial occupations and service occupations, but they were combined in 1962. A small, casual labor office was operated as an extension of the industrial office. In late 1962 a separate youth and student office was opened in the city. At the time it was the only one of its kind in the country, and it was a forerunner of the Youth Opportunity Centers which came into being years later.

From a statistical point of view there were approximately 83 staff members in the line operation manning the two offices. During fiscal 1962 the two offices together made 30,963 placements. There were 78,800 new applications taken, and there were 10,595 counseling interviews reported. In the commercial and professional office, a productivity study revealed that in calendar year 1962 there were an average of 49.7 personnel equivalents in the office, including supervisory and clerical staffs. Placements made during that same period numbered 6,161. Each staff member, then, produced 124 placements during the year, or a little better than ten placements per month. (In comparison, the average number of placements per staff member during calendar year 1970 was 74, approximately six per month.)

It is interesting to note here that one of the reasons used in arguing for installation of the national Employment Service Automatic Reporting System (ESARS) in 1970 was that placement and counseling figures included only local office "transactions" and did not necessarily relate to transactions with individual human beings. In other words, an individual could come into the office once, twice, or twenty times, and the statistical record showed only that an application was received, or a counseling interview occurred, or a placement was made; it did not show that all of these transactions involved the same individual or that a single individual required numerous transaction encounters and was still unable to obtain a job. Similarly, the same person — a domestic worker, a temporary clerical worker, a casual worker of any kind — may have been placed a number of times during the reporting period. ESARS was designed to correct some of this statistical distortion by indicating not only the number of transactions but the number of individuals served.

But even today when administrators discuss the activities of the employment service, they are likely to quote placement transaction figures. It should be understood that the employment service has yet to devise a reporting system that would allow adequate analysis of the *quality* of jobs, the occupational span, or the range of concentrations in which job orders and placements occur. Whether by intent or default — and despite two computerized systems — this kind of information is continually obscured.

It was in this context that the local employment service office operated in the early 1960s. And it was through the doors of that institution, with its particular mandate and orientation, that the unemployed San Franciscan came for help.

The Local Employment Service Office in the Early 1960s

The job seeker who came to the San Francisco local office entered a large, barn-like area in which a wall-to-wall counter separated the small public lobby from the much larger agency area. Behind the counter stood row upon row of metal desks at which interviewers sat facing the public area. The lobby itself was sparsely furnished and uninviting. In one part were rows of straight-backed metal chairs, arranged as in a lecture room, with individuals sitting in them starring at the counter. (Staff workers sometimes referred to this area as the "bull pen.") It was in this area that applicants waited to be called by interviewers. With the exception of a few posted civil service announcements, little information was displayed. The lobby was devoid of anything colorful or comfortable for the public; there was nothing to soften the impact of gun-metal gray bureaucracy.

The job seeker waiting in the lobby or standing in line at the counter marked "Reception" watched as the interviewers at their desks talked on the telephone, chatted with a neighbor at another desk, laughed with each other, walked about, or fussed with papers. As he waited . . . and waited . . . the job seeker was overcome with impatience. His anger was reflected in his face, in his whole demeanor. Its target was those persons behind the counter who "had it made." "They" had forgotten what it was to be unemployed or more likely had never known. Already the job seeker had waited through a long line to pick up application papers — probably on a previous day. This was his second trip.

As he waited to be called, he was chafed by "their" indifference. He was sure, watching, that most of "them" were doing absolutely nothing to earn their paycheck . . . the great civil service boondoggle. Filled with envy of "their" employment and security, he raged at "their" power to do him well or ill, to dispense jobs. Damn "them," it was his taxes that paid "their" salaries! But he knew that when his name was called, he would play out "their" game — a "con" game — because he dared not express what he really felt. The price of telling "them" off was too high, his need for the job "they" controlled too great.

Anyone who has worked in a public employment office has heard endless variations of such thoughts expressed aloud by unhappy job seekers who could not control their frustrations, their sense of indignity, and the intensity of their need.

Spaced along the counter which divided the office area from the lobby where three or four interviewers, each with one person in front of him. But there was a long line of applicants waiting at that section of the counter marked "Reception." The job seeker seated in the "bull pen" had been *there* before. The man behind the counter had asked him a few questions, had given him some papers to fill out, and had told him to return on this day and time to "Window D." The applicant was still a little angry about that first encounter with the receptionist. He had a little speech all worked out about what kind of work he could do and what kind of job he was looking for, but the man behind the counter had cut him short; he just gave him those papers to fill out and told him to come back.

The job seeker waited to be called by the woman at Window D. He watched what went on at that window, thinking once again about what he wanted to say. But this too looked like a fast operation. The woman behind the counter did most of the talking; the applicants seemed to say very little. He concluded that this Window D was not going to be the place where he could talk over his problems about work and get some advice. For that he needed to sit down with someone who had time to listen.

He had noticed that occasionally someone from behind the counter came out to the lobby and called the name of some applicant from the lobby. That seemed to be the only way an outsider could get behind the counter and to a desk.

After a long wait, the job seeker was called to Window D by the woman behind the counter. She asked him questions about what work he had done — in detail. Why had he left his jobs? What was he doing during the few years he had forgotten to list on his application papers? After asking the questions and making a few notes, the woman behind the counter told him that his occupational code was "shipping and receiving clerk." She said she would check job openings in that code, and she looked over a list on her desk. She told him there were no job openings, gave him an identification card, and told him he would be called if something turned up in his code. She advised him to return once a month to keep his application active.

"Next, please."

And the interview was over. But the man didn't want a job as a shipping and receiving clerk. He had been trying to get into something better, and he had been studying to prepare himself for a better job. He wanted to talk it over with someone to find out how to break into the new field. But he never got past the counter. He even tried to get a glimpse of the jobs on the woman's list, but she tipped it so he couldn't see it.

The job seeker had made two trips to the employment service office, he had wasted three hours, and he was no better off than when he began . . . except that now he was angry and discouraged.

Such was the picture of the typical job seeker at the typical employment service office. The reception line at the counter was the place where the public flow first came in contact with the agency. To move through the line took an average of half an hour during the busy part of the day, sometimes even longer. There are innumerable stories about high officials coming to see the manager of a local office and being forced to shuffle through the line. And there are stories of individuals with personal appointments with staff members having to step inside the public phone booth in the lobby to telephone the staff member behind the counter in order to get his attention. Less humorous but more frequent were the instances of individuals coming into the lobby and waiting through the line only to find that they were in the wrong office. They may have suspected they were in the wrong office when they walked in, but there was simply no one to ask without waiting in line. Even employers got trapped in the line on rare occasions — an unforgivable slight — and interviewers who expected a visit from an employer often took elaborate precautions to snatch him inside, bypassing the line.

There was no way for an applicant to bypass the line. In order to obtain a copy of a state form, such as the state personnel application form which was supplied to all state offices, the job seeker had to wait through the line. The office made no effort to provide any kind of express service. No one from the office ever stepped into the lobby for any purpose other than to call out a name.

The reception line led to the counter, which stood as a rampart, a boundary that defined the combat areas. It protected and defended the public agency from assault and harrassment, from the public it served, from "they" — the enemy.

At the same time, the pressures on the inside of the counter mounted during the course of the day. The receptionist listened to an anxious woman who needed reassurance or to a youngster who had never sought work before and wanted advice. In each instance the receptionist had to decide which behavior would make him more or less "human": Should he take an extra minute or two with the frightened woman or the raw youngster, or should he instead bow to the growing irritation of the man at the rear of the line who would have to wait even longer if he yielded to the appeal? The receptionist was constantly uncomfortable about such conflicts; they presented dilemma he could not resolve. He could only protect himself by trying to feel nothing, by trying to reduce the public to a mass of indistinguishable figures he needed to dispose of as quickly and courteously as possible. A little sign saying "Courtesy is contagious" was glued inside his station. Inevitably, the public became "they," the potentially hostile enemy.

The arrangement, the stance of the agency, the setting . . . every aspect of the initial encounter soured the air. The message of the agency was one of arrogance, of contempt for the convenience and state of mind of the job seeker. It conveyed the authoritarian attitude that what the agency had to give was available only to those individuals who behaved appropriately. Most of those who came in the door looking for help left with nothing.

Employees behind the counter were often disheartened, too. They knew the agency had little to give — many fewer jobs than applicants for them. They felt the stifling influence of the office atmosphere as they struggled to develop a meaningful encounter with job seekers. In many cases these essentially decent human beings who worked at various points inside the counter tried to build little islands of warmth, of human exchange, of kindness and helpfulness. But everything operated against the success of their efforts.

The picture is grim but not exaggerated. Not every job seeker reacted the way the subject of this narrative did. The line was not always long. The air was not always charged with anger and frustration. But neither is this picture an isolated or rare moment. Similar situations were experienced in offices all across the country by hundreds of thousands of human beings who encountered the bureaucracy of the employment service. And similar events were everyday occurrences for thousands of workers within the employment service.

Such incidents were not intended. No one planned to make a job seeker angry. And those workers behind the counter were *not* wasting time talking; nor were they ignoring the waiting public. They were working . . . and working hard. The unhappy end result was not intended or planned. But it happened. It happened because such a result was the inevitable spinoff of the employment service "standard operating procedures." Those procedures prescribed, step by step, what each employee was to do and how each job seeker was to be treated.

To begin with, the receptionist behind the counter was a qualified professional. The line was made up primarily of individuals looking for work. The receptionist screened the applicants, answered questions, handed out forms, and made appointments. Those job seekers who had previously registered and who had obtained identification cards were checked against a list of occupations in current demand. Few applicants matched the demand list. Those who did not were advised that there were no jobs for them; their identification cards were updated, and they were sent on their way. Those few applicants whose assigned occupational codes matched those on the demand list were routed for an interview with the appropriate placement interviewer.

First-time applicants were given colored application cards — salmon for veterans, yellow for women, white for men — and scheduled to return for a completion interview. Depending on the heaviness of traffic and the availability of staff, the completion interview could take place within the hour or could be delayed for as long as a week. A good receptionist had a working knowledge of the office, its various functions, its programs, and its staff specialties. He used that knowledge to answer questions and schedule interviews. He was also called upon to respond to a variety of questions concerning other agencies, various state programs and laws, agency procedures, and forms. The receptionist was evaluated on the basis of his ability to keep the line moving quickly while maintaining his "cool," despite the pressure of a long line of applicants.

The completion interviewer, most often located at the counter station (the lady at Window D), reviewed the work application form which had been completed by the applicant. The interviewer asked questions to clarify any information which had been omitted or inadequately supplied, made the necessary corrections, and filled in the gaps in the work history portion of the form. The major function of the completion interviewer was to appraise the job seeker's work history and education in order to assign a code number from the *Dictionary of Occupational Titles*. This coding actually began the process of matching qualified applicants to job orders by the file search method.

Depending on budgetary considerations, the time allocated for the completion of an application card varied from ten to fifteen minutes. At the end of the completion interview, the interviewer had several options regarding the disposition of the job seeker.

First, the interviewer had a demand list. These were jobs which were available but which could not be filled by a search of the applicant file. If the interviewer's appraisal of the job seeker matched a job or jobs on the demand list, he could refer the applicant to the desk which had responsibility for the occupation or industry designated — provided, of course, that the employment service interviewer at the desk was comparatively free.

Second, if the job seeker fell into one of several special categories, he could be referred to the desk concerned with that category. For example, an applicant with a physical handicap might be scheduled for an interview with the "special placement interviewer," a regular journeyman interviewer whose responsibilities included assessing each handicap for its occupational relevancy, "selling" employers on hiring the handicapped, and representing the agency in community programs for the handicapped. An applicant whose age militated against finding a job might be referred to the "older worker specialist" who had special duties in that area. These duties included providing his clientele with information about industry practices regarding the older worker, acting as an advocate for older workers to employers, and cooperating with community groups concerned with the older worker. Finally, those applicants who were veterans might be referred to the "veterans employment representative," who could help veterans understand reemployment rights and other benefits provided by law. This special interviewer was responsible for reviewing local office procedures to ensure that veterans were accorded preferential treatment in job referrals, as provided by law.

Third, if the job seeker indicated that he was uncertain of his occupational choice or if he was faced with the need to change occupations, he was referred to an "employment counselor." The counselor's mission was to assess all the skills of the labor market. Often this required testing and additional interviewing before a plan could be outlined to help the job seeker reach whatever occupational goal he and the counselor had agreed upon. The plan might involve additional schooling, some kind of stopgap work for an interim period, or a complete redirection in the kind of work sought. As aids in the process the counselor used approved aptitude test batteries, occupational guides provided by the research and statistics unit, and occupational information provided by the Labor Department. He was required to conduct and record his counseling interviews on special forms according to rigid guidelines.

If none of the options above seemed suitable for the applicant, the completion interviewer would advise the applicant that there were no job openings to suit his qualifications. The job seeker was then issued a coded identification card and told to return in thirty days if he was still unemployed in order to keep his name in the active file. He was cautioned that the office referred individuals to jobs on the basis of a search of the active files, and so there was no advantage for him to visit the office more frequently than once a month. The message was clearly: "Don't call us; we'll call you." This was the option most frequently used by the completion interviewer.

It should be remembered that the "special" interviewers mentioned above usually had no specialized outside training for the positions they held. They were called "specialists," but they acquired the title by virtue of a one-week in-service training program conducted by the employment service. The method for selecting special interviewers or "counselors" for this training program was somewhat haphazard. In the main it consisted of having the supervisory staff select from the office workers those who were to receive the training.

It might be well to digress from the description of staff duties in order to provide a bit of background information for those not thoroughly familiar with employment service operations and terminology. Perhaps the most important term is "placement." A placement could be counted by the agency *only* if the agency had an open job order listed which resulted in the selection, referral, and hiring of an applicant. All four elements must have been present: job order, selection, referral, and hire. This meant that a "match" which occurred because an interviewer "developed" a job for an applicant did not count as a placement; the open job order did not exist. Also, no placement was counted if an applicant was referred to an employer as a result of the listing of a clerical opening, for example, but was hired instead as a laboratory assistant. No placement was counted in cases where an applicant was referred to a job, where someone else was hired and then immediately fired, and where the original referral was then hired. This was considered a new job opening which was not placed with the employment service. Numerous other examples of activities which were not "placements" could be cited. Even in a case where the interviewer referred an applicant to a company because the company was known to hire workers with certain qualifications, the resulting hire could not be counted as a placement if no specific job order existed. In fact, giving labor market information to an applicant which may have been of crucial value to him in obtaining work was not a reportable activity (and was still not reportable as late as 1973).

Still another aspect of the criteria used for placement reporting had to do with very short-term jobs. For example, a single day's work cleaning a house, or babysitting, or performing other casual labor was considered a placement because all four elements were present. It is true that a distinction was made between placements on jobs lasting more or less than three days, but whenever gross placement figures for the employment service were quoted, these one-day jobs were included.

(Some of these problems in the placement count method were subsequently corrected by the employment service, but in the early 1960s — the period of concern here — this was the operative reporting system.)

An understanding of what constituted a countable placement is important because it had a direct relationship to the manner in which employment service offices operated. One of the factors which exterted the most influence on the daily activities of the staff and shaped the direction of the office was the unit time budgetary system. Under this system, each countable activity was equated to a time unit. Countable activities were those for which there was a document; e.g., a work application, a job order, a referral to a job, a counseling interview, or a placement. The most important unit time related to the number of placements made. It was with the placement count that the local office earned its staffing time. A drop in placements meant a loss of staff. Usually the loss of staff was from among the hourly employees, but every person in the office, from manager to clerk, was influenced by this system. Of course, the number of available staff members determined to a great extent how hard each worker had to labor in order to complete the office work load. Thus, the unit time system, although it did not result in a financial gain or loss to individual interviewers, did act as a strong incentive or threat. This is particularly interesting in view of the discussion in government circles about the value of financial incentives in government service institutions for influencing both quantity and quality of performance.

A placement interviewer was assigned to handle all transactions related to a particular group of occupations, or in some cases, to an entire industry. His primary function was to assess the job openings which he received and fill them with qualified applicants. On occasion he might attempt to develop a job opening for a particularly salable applicant by calling employers who he knew hired individuals with skills possessed by the applicant. He would then convince the employer that the applicant should be considered for a position, whether such a position had been listed or not. This process was called "job development" at that time (although the term has since been used in quite a different application related to employment of the disadvantaged). Very little job development took place, since it was not satistically a placement and did not provide the office with budgetary returns.

The placement interviewer took job orders from the employer by telephone and recorded the data on a job order form. He drew the pertinent information from the employer and on occasion advised him about prevailing wage rates and the number and quality of applicants available. Then the interviewer assigned an occupational and industrial code to the order and filed it in his job order box. Those work applications which carried occupational codes that fell within his realm were also routed to him so he could file them by code. His primary task was to match the applicant file against the job order file (using the occupational codes), select one or more of the "best" qualified applicants, contact each one by phone or mail, and provide the applicant with a referral card and whatever information was necessary to apply for the job. The placement process was characterized by these basic elements or activities: obtain information, code, file, match, select, and refer.

Another time-consuming element of his job consisted of verification. He had to maintain continuous contact with the employer to determine whether or not the referred applicant was hired and whether the job was still open. Every phone call, every movement required some kind of paper work. Clerical and reporting details were overwhelming and endless, although in some ways they were necessary. If the placement interviewer became ill, for example, it was essential that another interviewer be able to pick up at the exact point of the placement process.

The competence of the placement interviewer depended more or less upon the degree to which he could complete a match. At his best, he was a skilled, knowledgeable, and persuasive broker who knew the hiring staff of a number of employers and had developed some credence with them. At his poorest and least experienced, he required little more understanding than a desk file clerk in order to go through the motions of his job. If he remained on the same occupational desk over a period of time, he often developed sophisticated insights into the variables within an occupational group. This was his most valuable asset, and that knowledge was usually stored in his head. He knew the hiring practices — overt and covert — of the group of employers with whom he dealt. He knew their preferences, and he knew their prejudices. However, this knowledge was usually limited to those employers and those jobs which were listed with the employment service. Since this often represented only a tiny segment of the total jobs in that occupation, even the experienced placement interviewer tended to develop a kind of tunnel vision in his view of the marketplace. These limitations were often exacerbated by frequent staff changes which reduced the competency offered by a desk to little more than filling out the job order forms, taking messages, and making simple and obvious matches.

While employees were trained to perform the details of their tasks and to complete forms, there was little attempt to develop broad knowledge and understanding of the labor market and its complexities or to gain intimate knowledge of the local scene. There was extensive drill on the use of the *Dictionary of Occupational Titles* and the *Standard Industrial Classifications* because these were the daily tools. But training in the wider view was brief, formal, and cursory. It provided staff with little more than a general understanding about the process of arriving at unemployment figures. The only information regarding the current state of the labor market was a monthly bulletin distributed to each employee. It was prepared by the research and statistics staff and simply presented gross statistics on employment by industry, together with standard unemployment rate figures.

None of the materials provided by state or federal governments — including the monthly bulletin — offered any help to the interviewer who wanted to learn how to assist that large group of applicants who were *not* placed by the office. These unplaced job seekers were in the majority by a great margin. But the interviewer could do little to help them. Some information about occupations was available in the form of occupational guides, prepared at periodic intervals by the research and statistical section, and the federal *Occupational Outlook Handbook.* However, these were designed as tools of the employment counselor, and the majority of the staff had neither the time nor the inclination to acquaint themselves with the material.

No formal plan existed to encourage the staff to acquire any labor market information beyond that which was absolutely necessary to perform their own particular tasks in the matching operation and in the completion of agency forms and statistical information. And since no part of the placement function included a requirement to give information about the marketplace, no information was gathered or provided to the interviewer by the agency, except that periodically individuals in the local office prepared a summary of prevailing wage rates in certain occupations in order to make it possible for interviewers to respond to employer requests and to the requirements of the unemployment insurance program. As a consequence of this policy, when an interviewer was talking to an applicant for whom he did not have an opening, he was totally without resources to offer the job seeker. He had no questions to ask, no information to give, and no suggestions to proffer.

Another area of responsibility in the local office had to do with employer relations. Normally, one or more interviewers had the title of "employer relations representative." This person was assigned to the employer visiting program and made regularly scheduled visits to selected employers who hired the majority of the work force — the major market employers. The employer relations representative attempted to sell the employment service to the employer and gathered data about changes in the work force, together with projections of future employment trends. One of the sales tools used in this effort was a program called the "test selected applicant." The employment service office negotiated agreements with employers whereby the office would conduct aptitude and proficiency testing for the employer to be used in the selection of applicants for job openings. Information gathered by the employer relations representative was placed on an employer record card in the local office.

The foregoing describes the most important functions of the front line staff in the local office and the model by which the basic placement and counseling processes were performed. There were infinite small variations in procedures and staff assignments at various times in different offices. In smaller offices, for example, the completion of the work application might have been part of the placement interviewer's function. Unfortunately, for the staff behind the counter — and for the unemployed job seeker in front of it — this bureaucratic, manual model for an employment office was based on myth and bore little relationship to the real world of work.

Behind the Scene: Administration

The specific office of concern here was an office in San Francisco. In reality, it was two offices, consolidated into one for purposes of discussion. Each of the two offices was staffed by some forty persons. Most of them were career employees, employment security trainees, or employment security officers I (the title of the career journeyman). In order to qualify for the state written and oral examination for a career appointment, an individual must have obtained a college degree within the previous five years. Another group of individuals — called "employment and claims assistants" provided the offices with hourly, seasonal employees, and allowed for flexibility of staffing to meet the variations in demand which occurred throughout the year.

The agency's experience with the employment and claims assistant category was an interesting one. These individuals were hourly employees who served when needed, were subject to arbitrary layoff when work loads went down, and were limited in the number of hours they were permitted to work in one year. The classification did not require more than a high school diploma, and the qualifying written examination was far less complex than the one administered for the career employment security trainee position. The employment and claims assistants were also permitted to qualify for the career examination by substituting hours worked in the employment service for the college education requirement. In principle, these assistants were supposed to be relegated to the simpler tasks in the office. In fact, many proved to be among the most skilled and competent employees, and efforts were often made to retain their services beyond the nine-month-per-year limit imposed by regulations. More than one top administrator came into the agency through the alternate route offered by the employment and claims assistant classification. This positive experience with noncredentialed staff undoubtedly helped predispose administrators in the California employment service to welcome and expand on the New Careers concept when it came along some years later. The experience also helped mold agency attitudes which did not agree with those of the California State Personnel Board and which led the agency to seek changes in specifications to permit the hiring of more minority workers. There was a substantial body of evidence to indicate that the college degree did not ensure competency in the manpower field, and that invidivuals could be trained on the job to perform in a highly professional manner.

For each function performed by the local office, the central office of the agency provided a line-item manual which reflected state and national policy and which provided precise how-to-do-it instructions. There were separate manuals for completion, counseling, order taking, selection, referral, employer visiting, supervision, clerical operations, and each of the special applicant groups. Every step was described; every contingency was provided for. A constant flow of amendments to the manual involved the interviewer in an endless task of filing revisions in order to keep the manual current. The interviewer learned quickly that the manual was quite literally "the Bible" of the agency; it was the fountain of all wisdom and authority, without which he would be lost.

(One anecdote illustrates the degree of dependency upon the manual which permeated the agency. At a meeting of state employment service staff officials in 1963, the subject under discussion was the preparation of the agency for its role in the event of a nuclear attack. Staff members from the employment service section — all supervisors with statewide responsibilities — were asked to consider which of all employment service records they regarded as most important and necessary to be preserved by microfilming and safely stored so they would be readily available after a nuclear attack. The concensus was that above all else the manuals should be preserved as the critical tool. Some consternation arose concerning the problem of keeping the microfilmed manuals abreast of the almost daily amendments, but those in attendance soon reassured themselves that at least one of California's 120 local offices would remain intact and be able to provide an up-to-date manual. The specter of operating from a noncurrent manual after the holocaust had been laid to rest.)

Interviewers were supervised by a line supervisor — an employment security officer II — who obtained his position through the promotional examination process. The line supervisor was responsible for five to eight interviewers in a particular function, such as a counter operation or placement unit. The major part of his job consisted of evaluating check sheets for quality control — a continuous schedule for examination of all documents to determine whether the interviewers were precise, accurate, conforming to the manual, and supplying the clerical entries. The supervisor was also concerned with traffic flow, personnel management, on-the-job training of new personnel, and transmitting information and instructions to and from upper echelons. Next to violating the instructions in the manual, the greatest error the interviewer could make was to bypass his immediate supervisor and rupture the bureaucratic channels.

Depending upon the size of the office, additional levels of supervision may have been present in the local office. An employment security officer III might have been in charge of the entire section, and an employment security officer IV may have been present as operation supervisor. In any case, the office manager was the highest officer in the local office. He was responsible to a field supervisor. Just as in all other instances, the manual which governed the behavior of the office manager was rigid and constraining. There was literally no way for a manager to experiment, to innovate, or to change anything. Any departure from the norm required approval from higher echelons. Nothing in the official climate encouraged a manager to take chances on untried solutions to whatever problems might exist in the office.

It was true, also, that almost without exception the manager had been with the agency for many years and had laboriously worked his way through the various promotional steps by conforming to the rules; there would be little inclination left to challenge the "state of the art." The manager's main concern was to reconcile the number of staff hours used with the number of budgeted hours allocated. Much of the manager's time was devoted to satisfying the endless demand for reports required by the agency and maintaining contacts with various entities in the community, such as personnel associations. Of course, the manager was always concerned with the analysis of local office statistics, particularly with that most important statistic — the number of placement transactions made during the month.

Although the atmosphere between the staff and the supervisors in the office was friendly and informal — everyone was on a first-name basis — the relationships consisted essentially of giving orders, criticizing, and directing. Suggestions for short-cuts, new ideas, or questions about the validity of any function were neither encouraged nor welcomed, except in a very narrow arena. To involve the staff in the decision-making process was unheard of. The goal of the supervisors was to ensure that the staff did exactly what the manual prescribed, as quickly as possible, and with proper attention to the clerical aspects of the job. The ideal was a smooth, undeviating, well-ordered operation, exactly as dictated by the manual. As a result, an inordinate amount of supervisory effort and time went into concern about minor personnel infractions: a three-minute tardiness, failure to sign in or out, a few extra moments for coffee breaks.

Nevertheless, the office functioned in a reasonably well-ordered manner and with a minimum of disruption, just as did similar offices in every community in the country. This was true despite the wavering, uneven pattern of activity in the office which reflected the changing nature of the job market.

What were some of the realities that attended this process? What were the behind-the-scenes facts known by the staff? What pressures were exerted on the staff?

It must be remembered that the employment service is a public office. By mandate, it cannot restrict its flow of traffic or business. It cannot select its clientele. Even in those offices which are separated by occupational groupings or geographic boundaries, any person has the right to apply for a job in any office, whether or not he technically belongs there and whether or not he is "placeable." By definition, then, the relationship between supply (the job seeker) and demand (the job opening) is uncontrolled and uneven. In a generally tight market when unemployment is particularly low, or in situations where sudden shortages occur, or when new occupations emerge from new technologies, there are more jobs than there are applicants for them. When this condition persists, the marketplace has a strong tendency to correct itself. Employers redesign jobs, lower their qualifications, raise wages, or do their own training. Vocational schools open and colleges redesign courses. These and other mechanisms come into play and act as stabilizers. During these periods when there is an adequate supply of workers, the employment service office may be inundated with orders. An employer may place the same order with every private agency in town as well as purchase an advertisement in the newspaper.

If shortages of workers persist, they often reflect a malfunction of the marketplace or a calculated manipulation of the market. In some cases, as in the medical profession or in some unionized crafts, shortages are artificially maintained in order to elevate income. In other cases, such as the skilled clerical and domestic occupations often called "women's jobs," an apparent shortage of workers more accurately indicates a high turnover rate resulting from low wages or undesirable characteristics of the job. Every employment service office has experience with unfilled job orders for highly skilled stenographers at the equivalent of a dishwasher's wage, and with the endless number of "live-in housekeeper" job orders that remain perennially unfilled.

Each of these factors exerts some effect on the operation of the employment service office. One graphic example of such effects occurred in an area that had seen a sudden and phenomenal growth of industry. New factories were coming in and placing their orders with the employment service. According to the staff, the flood of orders was so heavy during one period that most of the office staff was shifted to the order processing side of the office. They were so busy manning the telephones that there was hardly time to deal with those coming into the office to look for work. Orders went unfilled because there wasn't time or staff to go through those processes which would get the man and the job together. Just one year later, when a recession set in, the counter stations were so filled with individuals looking for work that most of the staff had to be shifted to that side of the office where they could take work applications. And of course, many job orders went unfilled because there wasn't time or staff to go through those processes which would get the man and the job together.

In both instances the interviewer could not simply hang up the telephone with a job order in hand and walk over to the waiting applicant who might fill it — because there was no provision in the manual for such action. Instead, the interviewer had to take the job order over the telephone, file the job order, and then go through a file search of coded application cards. Technically, he was not supposed to speak to a man who might be waiting for a job; he could only address himself to an application which the man might have filled out previously and which had been properly coded and inserted in the file. Even though these might have been semiskilled factory jobs where little selection and referral were necessary, the job openings could not openly be posted before the job seekers. First they had to be buried in the files before they could be dug up from the files and finally offered to the applicants.

This situation where there is an overabundance of job openings is the exception rather than the rule. The most common experience of the employment service everywhere is that there are far more persons looking for work than there are jobs suited for them. The central, pervading way of life for most employment service operations is that the staff must say "no" to most individuals who come for a job referral.

Naturally, this is terribly frustrating for employment service workers, as well as for those who come to the employment service office looking for work. But it must be remembered that the role of the employment service — unlike that of other government services — is only that of a broker. If a person goes to the welfare office for welfare, it is within the power of that office to say "yes" or "no" to the applicant. If an individual goes to a bank for a loan, the bank can grant the loan or refuse it. But it is *not* within the power of the employment service to *give* anyone a job. That power belongs only to the employer. Nor can the employment service create a job if it doesn't exist. But for the most part, the public does not perceive this distinction. In the public eye the failure of the welfare office to provide a welfare payment and the failure of the employment service to provide a job are equated. They are looked upon as similar rejections.

This was especially true in the early 1960s.

At the reception counter, for example, a large part of the traffic consisted of job seekers who had previously filed their applications and were checking in for a job. Some made the trip every day. Their visit to the office began and ended at the waiting counter with a one-minute exchange, during which the receptionist was required to play out the script that required him to at least give the appearance of checking job openings in order to assure the man that there was no job opening for a warehouseman. (Let's assume that was the applicant's job classfication.) What the receptionist did not tell the job seeker was that the last job for a warehouseman was listed two weeks earlier, that it had been a substandard job, and that five men before him had been looking for the same kind of work that same day. Nor would the receptionist advise the applicant about where to go and what to do in order to find his own job, since his chances of finding one through the office were so slim.

This whole process gave the impression, whether intended or not, that the office had jobs available but gave them only to those individuals who qualified. For most of the applicants, even the impression was a fraudulent one because the office did not have the jobs. But the great disaster, in human terms, was that this false impression placed the failure of the transaction squarely on the shoulders of the job seeker. He was made to feel that *he* was lacking, not the office and not the job market. He was unintentionally led to the assumption that because he was not selected for the job, he must have some personal inadequacy for which he alone was responsible. And if the applicant was black, he invariably reasoned that there was indeed a job, but it was given to someone else who was a white man.

If the applicant felt cheated by this unhappy charade, the staff workers, too, received little in the way of satisfaction. They were frustrated and angry. A day of such fruitless and destructive encounters was enough to send one home weary and discouraged.

The completion interviewer, too, knew that far more than half of the application cards which he so laboriously reworked and coded would be counted and filed and never looked at again. While every application card was an implied promise that the time-consuming paper work would have some beneficial result, the completion interviewer knew that in most cases the promise would be broken. But he played out his script (dictated by the manual) to obscure this reality. He would rise from his desk, walk over to the placement desk, check the orders, ask the interviewers a few questions, and then return to report what he already knew before he left his desk: There were no "suitable" openings for the applicant.

For those involved, the process was indeed frustrating, especially when those paradoxical situations arose which became so well known to the employment service staff. For example, many applicants simply could not fill out an application card properly. Conscientious interviewers would run well over the allotted fifteen minutes helping an applicant put together a coherent work history, asking questions and adding material to make the card acceptable for office records — and for the critical eye of the supervisor. Misspelling would be corrected. Where the job applicant wrote the word "labor" to describe a job, the interviewer would secure enough information to elaborate: "Worked fork lift; supervised five men." The interviewer would carefully reconstruct a period on the work history which the applicant left blank. Then this meticulously prepared card would go into the active application file, possibly to remain untouched until it was purged as inactive. In the meantime, the applicant, still in need of a job, left the office and walked across the street to a small manufacturing company. He filled out a work application form in the same inadequate way he had at the employment service. When the personnel manager of the company reviewed the application, he was unimpressed with the term "labor" describing a period of employment. He needed a person with some knowhow who could work a forklift and who had some supervisory experience. Furthermore, those gaps in the applicant's work history were suspect because he may have spent that time in jail or in a mental institution. The application was filed away; the job seeker did not get the job for which he was well qualified. This example is not fantasy. A survey conducted at about that same time with the personnel offices of San Francisco area hospitals disclosed that the most often repeated explanation for not hiring employment service referrals was the poorly completed application card.

In the example, the completion interviewer had obviously had enough training or experience to know how the application card should read in order to present the most favorable picture of the job seeker. But there was not time, or bureaucratic leeway, or outlined agency mission that allowed (or encouraged) the interviewer to provide the job seeker with a copy of the reworked application or to teach him how to fill one out properly elsewhere. Instead, the employment service had a perfectly completed application card in its file; the applicant had no job and no increased skill in obtaining one. There was simply no incentive to help the applicant in this fashion, because even if he had gone across the street and *successfully* applied for that job, it would not have counted on the local office's placement statistics.

Still another problem area was the coding process. Completion interviewers often had a problem selecting the proper occupation code for an applicant. Most humans have a variety of skills and inclinations, not just one. And oftentimes individuals wanted the opportunity to try something different from what they had done in the past. But the allocation of an occupational code was determined by a combination of factors, including the nature of the longest held job, the highest skill obtained, and any formal training completed. Of all the possibilities for each applicant, only one code was selected — supposedly the one through which he could best be exposed to a job. According to the manual, if additional and unrelated skills were indicated or if the applicant expressed a desire to work in a different field, a skeleton application was to be completed and cross referenced to the major code.

In actual fact, the preparation of a secondary card was a nuisance to the completion interviewer, since little budgetary time was allocated to that function. Also, placement interviewers tended to ignore the secondary cards when making a file search, because they contained little information and always required a second step — looking up the primary card.

In addition, the coding process was a source of continuous — and legitimate — concern to the job seeker. He was eager to work, and he wanted exposure to a number of jobs so his opportunities could be increased. He frequently objected to the coding system and expressed concern that his willingness to learn and his acquired capabilities were not adequately represented within the limitations of the coding system.

Just as debilitating as the restrictions written into the standard operating procedures were the many "myths" of operation that permeated office activities. According to the law, veterans were to have preference on job referrals, and to ensure that preference, the salmon-colored veterans application cards were filed at the beginning of each occupational group. But the preference was mythical. The veteran employment representative knew that it operated only when there were large orders to fill. The interviewer who had an applicant in mind when he took a job order referred that applicant without regard to the rules. In reality, it was the employer who decided whether or not he wanted to consider a veteran.

Counseling was another myth. The counselor played out the rules of his game. His position in the office structure led the job seeker to assume that the counselor had both intimate knowledge of occupations and the power to manipulate local labor markets. In most cases this was grossly exaggerated. The counseling format was observed, and counseling plans were dutifully recorded, but very few plans were ever completed. Counseling programs were often based on the premise that the job seeker had a range of alternatives when the alternatives didn't actually exist.

The success of the employer relations program was always so questionable that it, too, belongs in the category of myth. Although the visits to employers were usually made at the prescribed intervals of time, in almost every case the employer relations representative found that his call was little more than a repetitious courtesy call. The large employers used job-matching mechanisms which were firmly established, or they had their own personnel offices where applications were taken directly from job seekers. Some were obliged to use union hiring halls by contractual agreement, and some had long-established relations with schools and private agencies. Those employers who made use of the public employment service for particular kinds of jobs did so in response to the twists and turns of the economy rather than as a result of any sales pitch by the local office. The program was also quite expendable. It was the only activity which the office manager could easily modify or even eliminate; the flow of applicants and jobs was beyond his control. As a result, whenever the office was under pressure or was behind in any phase of its work, the employer relations program was the first to be curtailed. However, studies of the statistical relationship between employer visits and the number of job openings showed very little correlation. (An undated study conducted by a state task force in 1970 showed the relationship between total employment, unemployment rates, total employer contacts, placements, and job openings received in California during a ten-year period. In 1961 employer visits were at their peak, nearly double those in 1966; yet the greatest number of job openings received was in 1966. In 1962 the commercial and professional office in San Francisco made 5,769 employer visits. The placement count for the same year was 7,333. In 1966 the same office made 883 employer visits — a drop of approximately 85 percent — but placements in 1966 were 6,564, a drop of only 10 percent.)

But the greatest chasm between reality and myth was in relation to the placement function. The most serious discrepancies were in regard to just how many of the applicants who came to the office actually obtained work and what kind of employers obtained their help through this process.

It should be stated at the outset that the labor exchange model which characterized the employment service in 1962 produced some excellent placement services, just as the different models of later years produced some good results. For that small number of individuals who successfully hurdled the obstacles between them and a friendly, first-name relationship with an interested and skilled placement interviewer, a very useful service was provided. There was a particular, almost uncanny talent that many placement interviewers developed which made it appear as if they snatched jobs out of thin air. By programming bits and pieces of seemingly irrelevant information into their heads, these interviewers developed an unerring sense of the match, a sure-fire instinct about which employer to phone in order to "sell" an applicant, or which applicant to send to a seemingly irascible employer.

The difficulty stemmed from the fact that only a small number of applicants who came to the office were able to get that kind of personal service. Expressed statistically, in 1962 the commercial and professional office in San Francisco averaged 124 placements per year for each staff equivalent or approximately 2.4 placements per staff member per week. This is not a definitive picture because staff equivalents included clerical, supervisory, and other staff not directly involved in the placement process. Nevertheless, the number of persons who might have had the opportunity to sit down with a placement interviewer for the kind of quality service that results in a good match was very small compared to the number who came into the office and expected such service. A later study disclosed that 86 percent of the applicants did not get jobs through the placement process.[1]

It was also a myth that the primary method for selecting and referring individuals to job openings was the file search. It was common practice to refer someone to a job because he happened to be in the office. Numerous studies have established that services performed by the office for applicants were far greater on the initial visit than on subsequent visits. Once the application

---

[1]Stanford Research Institute, *Pilot Study of Services to Applicants* (Stanford Research Institute, Palo Alto, 1967).

card was placed into the active file, the job seeker's chance of being contacted became more and more remote, unless the applicant happened to be endowed with unusual salability or scarce skills.

The claim that the office referred the "best qualified" applicant to the employer could hardly be supported by the facts. It was another myth. When job orders were difficult to fill because applicants with the stated qualifications were scarce, it was common practice to refer an individual even if his qualifications were only remotely related to those specified on the job order. At the same time, a single job order for a sales clerk (for example) compared against an active file of one hundred applicants — which was the most common relationship between job and applicant in low-skill jobs — was not likely to produce anything resembling a "best qualified" selection. The interviewer hardly needed to get through the names starting with A to make an "adequate" selection.

Numbers — the placement count — may not be mythical, but they can certainly be misleading. Most placement interviewers knew that the jobs which went into the placement count were real jobs but were predominantly of poor quality. Many times the job order box contained nothing but commission sales jobs or jobs with low pay and poor working conditions.

Recently two economists evolved a theory about the operation of the labor market which has gained considerable acceptance.[2] Called the "dual labor market theory," it contends that there are in reality two markets operating. One, the primary market, has the stable jobs with good pay, job security, and upward mobility. The other, the secondary market, operates in those occupations and industries where training is minimal and turnover is high and less costly. The secondary market is characterized by poor jobs, low pay, instability, and no job security. When one of the authors was asked to describe this secondary labor market in more specific terms, he said, "It is those jobs listed with the employment service." It is interesting that when workers in the employment service hear of this theory, they have an instinctive acceptance of it and begin to use the term "secondary labor market" without

---

[2]Peter B. Doeringer and Michael J. Piore, *Internal Labor Markets and Manpower Analysis* (Lexington, Massachusetts: D. C. Heath & Co., 1971).

requiring exact definitions; they have been dealing with it for a long time.

The placement interviewer in the office of the early 1960s may have had no theoretical formulation, but he had knowledge that what passed through his job order box — the placements he so assiduously sought — too often failed to provide him with a sense of accomplishment or usefulness, let alone provide a serious answer for the unemployed person. Most often the transaction did not require him to exercise that body of knowledge regarding the selection and referral process for which he was presumably trained. Too many of the jobs were on the very bottom of the quality scale and needed only a "body" which could just as easily have been obtained by posting the notice wherever the unemployed congregated.

In marked contrast was that moment when it all worked — when the job was worth filling, when it did answer the needs of the job seeker, when the interviewer played a significant role in the process, and when he could feel that he was of value to both employer and job seeker. His exuberance, his retelling of the events to his fellows at the coffee break, his excitement and obvious pleasure . . . all served to point up the rarity of such occasions and the futility of his usual activity.

The importance given to the placement count had insidious effects on all the activities of the interviewer and, by extension, on the role played by the employment service throughout the nation, particularly in the period prior to public consciousness about race discrimination. Picture the behavior of the receptionist toward a black applicant for a white-collar job. Whatever else the receptionist might have thought, the black man did not represent an easy placement, and his dismissal by the receptionist was very likely even more abrupt than usual. Picture the placement interviewer in the early 1960s taking an order from an employer for a well-groomed, high-class receptionist with typing skills. Searching the files, the interviewer's finger stopped on the application card of a qualified person. However, either by the address on the card, or the name of the applicant, or his own memory, or the unofficial code mark on the card, the interviewer became aware that the applicant was black. He had only to flick his finger and go to the next card to find an equally qualified white applicant. To do so did not require an inordinate degree of racial prejudice; it required only an awareness of the incentives. The possible rewards that went with referring the white applicant were a placement count and a satisfied employer who would call again. The possible punishments for referring the black applicant were a loss of the time spent, no statistical count, an angry employer who would not place an order again, and — despite the official agency policy against discrimination — something less than a gold star of approval from supervisors and fellow employees. To refer the black applicant under those conditions required an exceptionally strong commitment to racial equality.

Intrinsic in the system was always the pressure to satisfy the employer's needs. The employer wanted the most experienced and best trained worker who would be most acceptable in his enterprise. He needed to fill the job openings as quickly as possible. Of course, workers who fit such a description were those best able to find jobs on their own. The poor, the black, the traditionally excluded individual had the greatest need for some kind of intervention in his behalf if he was ever to open the doors to untraditional jobs and break into the primary labor market. But the employment service could function only as a broker. It had to please the employer if it was to retain his business and compete with other job-matching mechanisms.

Inevitably, the employment service provided underpinning for the hiring practices of the employers. It militated against the hard to place, the poor, the black, and the disadvantaged — despite the apparent provision for special services to certain groups of applicants. It was party to the exclusion of the minority work force from the full range of opportunity. And conversely, the employment service assured the secondary labor market employers of a continuing supply of low-priced, often black, work force.

The receptionist's curt dismissal of the black man, the interviewer's finger moving past the qualified black woman — duplicated thousands of times each day in the city — constituted (and still does) a social reality. The office then (and the office today) too often lagged well behind the conscience and the practices of the community. The office was under pressure to cater to the employing community's prejudices, its whims, and its collective philosophy. That these may have been in direct conflict with the goals of the nation, with the formal policies of the agency, with current knowledge of the job market, and with the morality of the staff was then (and is now) a root cause for the dilemma.

In a symbolic sense, that is the meaning of the counter. It not only protected the agency from the pressures of the job-seeking public, but it also diverted and absorbed the assault of those who were left out and thus acted as a buffer on behalf of a remote and aloof economic establishment.

CIRCA 1966:
Serving the Disadvantaged

During the first half of the decade of the 1960s, the counter in most employment service offices received a new coat of paint, but it remained. On both sides of the counter, however, drastic changes were taking place — in the American society and in the functions performed by the employment service. For one thing, the nation became concerned with its human resources and developed public programs to train — or retrain — its "manpower."

Manpower training programs began with the passage of the Manpower Development and Training Act (MDTA) in 1962. It provided that the program be jointly administered by the Department of Labor and the Department of Health, Education and Welfare. On the local scene, this meant that the employment service had the responsibility for selecting the occupations, selecting the trainees, placing them on a job after training, and keeping overall records. The education system had the responsibility for providing the training. The trainees received a weekly stipend while in training. For the first time, the employment service was required to engage in an activity designed to change one of the components of the marketplace, to manipulate the supply. To the employment service's original six-point program was added a seventh — training. Passivity regarding the market was at an end. "Facilitating the employment process" now meant something more than simply matching man to job. It meant changing the man to fit the job.

By 1966 when the ghetto office which will be described here was operative, MDTA had been amended, broadened, and refocused as a tool for the disadvantaged. Sixty-five percent of the resources available under the Act were committed to those who met poverty criteria. Additionally, the Economic Opportunity Act brought with it a new array of manpower training components such as Job Corps, Neighborhood Youth Corps, and Work Experience and Training — converted in 1967 into the Work Incentive Program (WIN) under an amendment to the Social Security Act. The Economic Opportunity Act also triggered a struggle on the national scene for control over which agency would deliver the programs. It was the contention of many in the antipoverty arena that the Department of Labor and its network of offices were too entrenched and moribund to make the attitudinal, procedural, and personnel changes required to deal successfully with the poor.

At the local level the power struggle had less meaning. Whether or not the employment service was responsible for administering any one of the discrete programs, it was always necessary for the local administrators to turn to the employment service office for recruitment of potential trainees, for assistance in design and execution, and for placement. The local office staff had to know about, have the forms for, and be able to make the fine point distinctions among manpower programs — which programs were available for which type of clients under which eligibility criteria? In addition, the national concern about the young resulted in the establishment of Youth Opportunity Centers in poverty communities across the country. These changes resulted in a tremendous proliferation of installations and of staff.

It is interesting to compare the concept of service that prevailed when the agency was essentially passive and focused on a simple match between man and job with the concept which came later. That first concept produced a language — definitions of what can be called the array of activities that constituted employment services. Essentially they were reception, completion, selection and referral, placement, verification, counseling, testing, employer visiting. Each had one meaning for the designers and a quite different meaning when hammered out at the counter. The shift to a concern for the disadvantaged brought a new lexicon of definitions of job descriptions and of umbrella words about what staff did on the job that might be called a manpower service. The new words included "outreach," "orientation," "intake," "assessment," "coaching," "selection and referral for training," "job development in a new sense," "intensive follow-up."

There were also big, encompassing words and phrases such as "supportive services" beginning to appear in the local offices. This term described everything from funded health examinations for trainees to scrounging a free meal for a hungry man. There were such terms as "employability development services" which designated that group of activities which would change a man's attitudes toward work and focus on those problems which prevented him from becoming employed even when a job was available. Each had a meaning to the designer and a quite different reality in the local office. Some concepts emerged out of actual experience. There was no way to deny to front-line staff that a great number of the disadvantaged clientele were found to have a relationship to work or training that was casual at best. But since the quality of jobs and training offered was normally designed to evoke something less than enthusiastic commitment, this was understandable if disappointing. Some concepts were propounded by representatives and spokesmen for the black community who assumed that black men in particular had long ceased to trust any agency of government and would need to be found in the streets and pool halls if manpower services were to be delivered to the intended target population. And so "outreach" became an activity.

A series of executive orders and administrative fiats attempted to redirect and restructure the operations of the agency nationally.

The Department of Labor adopted a human resources development concept — an *applicant* service, with special emphasis on serving the disadvantaged, for which additional staff positions were allocated to the states. The attempt was made to broaden the scope of the service, to transform it into a comprehensive manpower institution capable of meeting the employment related needs of that hitherto ignored segment of the unemployed. Instead of passively acceding to the exclusion of nonwhites from referral to jobs, the Department of Labor, with considerable trepidation and internal opposition, undertook to create a vehicle in the network offices to actively encourage the integration of the work force. The staff was urged to induce employers to abandon discriminatory hiring practices and to reduce those nonperformance requirements which had traditionally served to exclude minorities. Offices were directed to apply more rigorously the injunction against accepting discriminatory orders. Again, the focus shifted from accepting the marketplace as it was to aggressively seeking to change one of its components — the hiring practices of employers. Even the names of offices were changed, in many cases, to reflect the shift — from "Employment Service" to "Manpower Centers." This shift in focus met with wide resistance in many parts of the country.

There is little doubt that the new focus added further impetus to the already downward trend of orders and placements. Many employers were discouraged from placing their job orders with the employment service because they had no intention of abandoning their discriminatory hiring practices; others simply feared coming under the scrutiny of a public agency. It is possible that some employers gave up on the agency because they had poor service on their orders.

On the other hand, a new body of employers emerged who sought out the employment service *because* they were seeking talent in the minority work force, either because of an aroused social conscience or through government pressure. This presented the agency with a legal dilemma caused by the legislation and policy originally intended to overcome racial discrimination. There were, after all, prohibitions against taking a "discriminatory" order or designating race on an application card. How, then, was the black applicant to be singled out for referral? The dilemma was met by states and local offices in a variety of interesting ways. Some of the offices which had been less than assiduous in enforcing the rules when they were designed to *protect* minorities exhibited considerable ingenuity in devising ways of again circumventing the rules because those same rules could now operate *against* minorities. They found ways to allow the agency to serve those employers and applicants through such devices as establishing a minority specialist in every office, or locating employment service offices within the ghetto. This not only served to channel job and applicant so a match would be possible, but it had other far-reaching effects. Wherever such concentration and outreach activity took place, it tended to create considerable change in the agency, in its management style, and in the sensitivity of the staff. Those offices did indeed increase their capability to deal with the minority unemployed.

However, most state and local administrators, who were deeply committed to the broker role, sensed that the new emphasis threatened their legitimacy. They resisted the direction of the Department of Labor, denouncing "reverse discrimination" with the kind of energy that was scarcely evident when it was just "discrimination." That the aggressive advocate role for the poor remained largely theoretical was the charge made in a 1971 report prepared by the Lawyers Committee for Civil Rights and the Urban Coalition. The report was titled "Falling Down on the Job: The United States Employment Service and the Disadvantaged." The report, which received considerable national publicity, concluded that manpower training programs and the restructuring of the employment service to better serve the disadvantaged resulted only in add-on programs that did not intrinsically change the nature and commitment of the agency or the orientation of its staff. (The report is dealt with in more detail in Chapter 6.)

If the new direction of the agency caused some local offices to frantically resist change, it also allowed some forward-looking offices to see a great opportunity for innovation and service. Such was the case in the northern California agency, where the imagination and courage of administrators was unsurpassed and where the restructing and reorienting of a staff and services was most actively pursued.

New Directions in California and San Francisco

The responses of the northern California service to the nationally funded manpower programs were uncommonly aggressive and speedy. Despite the delineated, often narrow role generally assigned to state employment services by these funded programs, the northern California agency managed on several occasions to expand and reinterpret its role. A number of important, innovative concepts and programs emerged from experiments originating in the San Francisco Bay Area. Some of them had national impact.

The process by which the coastal region, particularly in San Francisco, converted itself cannot be examined without recalling some of the factors that played upon the consciousness of its leaders and its front-line staff prior to the national directive.

In late 1962, when the freedom riders and restaurant sit-ins were stirring the country — well before the burning of Watts, well before MDTA was fully operational or had changed direction, well before any national human resource development concept — the director of the California State Employment Service issued a letter, a copy of which was provided to every employee throughout the state. This rather uncommon method of communicating with staff implied the importance placed on the letter by the director. It announced a dramatic policy shift for the agency. Though a policy of nondiscrimination had been in effect since 1949, the letter declared that the California State Employment Service was now abandoning its passive position and embarking on a policy of actively and aggressively seeking the integration of the work force. It was placing itself in the position of alliance with the great civil rights movement. (It is important to note that the governor of California supported the direction taken by the agency head.) The letter declared that as the manpower arm of government, the agency was prepared to focus its resources on that segment of the work force which had been traditionally excluded.

The letter was followed by a series of implementing steps which included the establishment of a minorities program in each local office, centering around a minority specialist whose desk was to be the channeling device for placing qualified minority applicants and overcoming employer resistance. Central office training was developed and given to every person in the agency. In a courageous move, risking attack from the civil rights organization but with the permission of the Fair Employment Practices Commission, the department began maintaining racial statistics on such transactions as unemployment insurance claims, new job applicants, persons referred to jobs, applicants placed on jobs, and trainees enrolled in MDTA courses. Care was taken that such records would be originated in the local offices but would not remain there. There were two purposes in instituting racial data on state forms: first, to develop more information on the employment problems of minority workers, and second, to evaluate the effectiveness of the agency in serving these groups. This was the first focus on racial information in official documents since the period when racial designations were used to discriminate against minorities.

Instructions to local offices urged managers and staff to become involved in and responsive to the growing militancy in the black community and to offer assistance and cooperation to civil rights organizations. This was the first time the staff had ever been invited to step out of its traditional isolation. It was the first state agency in the country to take such a public position with its own staff. It reflected the political atmosphere in the governor's office, true, but even more importantly it made very plain to the entire agency the seriousness and extent of commitment on the part of the director and other policy makers. The effect of this change was dramatic and convulsive in all parts of the state. To much of the leadership and staff it was threatening; anger, consternation, and resistance resulted. There was then, as now, serious concern about the possible loss of job orders from employers. However, to those whose sympathies were aroused by the black struggle going on in the south and who had chafed under the arrogance and rigidity of the employment service, to those who had watched the discriminatory practices of the agency itself in silent disapproval, the director's position statement provided the underpinning for boldness and innovation.

One of the first activities undertaken by the agency in San Francisco, in open partnership with a civil rights group, serves as an example of the naivete with which both the civil rights groups and the agency approached the employment problems of the minority work force. An official of the National Association for the Advancement of Colored People (NAACP) who had participated in the minority advisory committee complained that employers insisted they could not find qualified black applicants. Assuming that there existed abundant numbers of unemployed blacks with high skills, a skill inventory system was devised which was to be conducted jointly by the California State Employment Service and NAACP. The inventory was intended to uncover, register, and refer these people to jobs. More than two thousand blacks were registered by a host of volunteers in six successive weekends. Literally dozens of interviewers from the public employment service volunteered their time. The results were something of a fiasco.

Registrants generally lacked placeable skills, and of those individuals the employment service attempted to reach and serve, only 127 job referrals were made, which resulted in only 30 placements. The experience caused much soul searching with the agency. Certainly, the illusion of easily found skills was dispelled. Beyond this, the survey pointed up the degree to which large numbers of unemployed, unskilled blacks were aliented from public agencies.

One factor which electrified the staff and the public and altered the stance of the hitherto isolated agency was the official form and the public announcement which said: "CSES-NAACP Skill Inventory." That both parties were willing to enter such a partnership publicly was something of a turning point. It brought an awareness to the leaders of the minority community that the agency could be used as an ally and a source of competent help. It also made the direction of the agency quite clear to the staff.

Another example of early daring which strongly affected the atmosphere in the local office occurred in 1963. The area labor market analyst who headed the staid research and statistics unit in the area office responded to the informational vacuum that existed about the black work force by assembling and publishing a document, distributed publicly, which analyzed the position of the minority work force in the Bay Area from 1960 census material. Stepping beyond the normal assigned duties of his job, he published the document without the blessings of the central office research section. There was no precedent for statistical racial focus anywhere in California, and there were hostile reactions from many research and statistics personnel throughout the state. However, the area manager supported the report, which was eagerly used by minority leaders. To the staff in the local offices in San Francisco, it was another step in the process of changing consciousness about where the agency was going and what it wanted from the staff.

Still another impetus came about because the agency engaged in a series of youth programs located in the poverty communities in San Francisco and other Bay Area communities. These were programs administered jointly with other agencies. In retrospect, the administrators felt that one of the sharpest turning points in their own awareness came as a result of these efforts when they saw their own all-white, middle-class staffs attempting to deal with the ghetto youth in the ghetto setting. It was then that they began to search for ways to circumvent the rigidity of specifications set by the civil service system in order to be permitted to hire more appropriate staff. One of the lessons learned from these interagency efforts was that programs operated in partnership present nearly insurmountable obstacles and produce little of value. Inevitably, the main brunt of responsibility fell on the employment service staff, which was the most vulnerable and exposed. Joint agency responsibility brought together conflicting styles and conflicting mandates, and the combined weight of all the involved bureaucracies fell most heavily upon the lowest point in the structure, the front-line interviewer.

The personal commitments and the leadership style of the top executive in any organization influences the results. So it was with the coastal area manager and his effect on the pioneering effort of the 1960s. He not only allowed but encouraged a good deal of innovation and experimentation in the Bay Area and he personally championed unpopular causes on behalf of the disadvantaged. It was he who bore the brunt of the invective from both individuals and from organized groups, but despite tremendous pressure, he never relented from his efforts to initiate programs or respond to needs that grew out of the minority struggle. It is not possible to understand the peculiar role of the northern California agency during the 1960s without acknowledging the enormous influence of the coastal area manager. The staff in the coastal area office reflected his personal commitments and leadership style. Those in the lower echelons felt that, despite inherent bureaucratic restraints, he would be supportive of efforts in this direction, just as he could be reasonably certain of the director's support.

In 1966, the administrative structure of the agency was essentially the same as it was in 1962, so far as the division of the state and the coastal area office was concerned. The administration of MDTA brought a flood of new front-line staff and new administrative functions to the coastal area office as well as to the central office in Sacramento, but the coastal area office was intact, and the leadership remained essentially the same and unified in purpose.

The popular wisdom in national manpower circles defined the restructuring of the delivery system as the key to solving manpower problems of the disadvantaged, and California shared this assumption. The California Legislature twice attempted to legislate an alternative system to the employment service. The first was in 1965 when an act was passed to establish the State Multi-service Center program. This legislation prescribed that centers be established in economically disadvantaged communities which would incorporate into one location and under the aegis of one administrative entity the combined resources of all people-oriented state agencies. Though each established agency would remain intact, each would provide a contingent of staff and programs to what was called a one-stop service center. State funds were allocated for administrative purposes. These allowed for the establishment of a State Service Center administrative agency, and they also allowed the centers to hire staff in addition to that provided by existing agencies. The Service Center manager and assistants were employed directly by the State Service Center program.

However, the facts were that there were actually only two state agencies providing a direct service to the public — the California State Employment Service and the Department of Vocational Rehabilitation. All of the other state agencies — the Department of Health, the Department of Education, the Department of Social Welfare — were administrative entities. The direct health, education, and welfare services were provided to the public by city and county agencies which were not part of the Service Center program. The Department of Corrections was a state agency, but duties of parole officers could hardly be regarded as a service to the unemployed. The Department of Vocational Rehabilitation had a limited program and budget for training and rehabilitating disabled persons. Eligibility for the rehabilitation program had been extended by a policy shift to include more disadvantaged persons under the category of "disabled."

To place this development in perspective, it should be noted that before the law creating State Service Centers was passed and operative, Adult Opportunity Centers had been funded and were operating to serve the population of the ghetto in San Francisco. These Adult Opportunity Centers were part of the employment service network in the city and were designed to give assistance to the disadvantaged in their attempts to obtain employment. Interviewers in the Adult Opportunity Centers were already taking advantage of the expanded eligibility rules under the rehabilitation program as an additional resource for their applicants. In the process they were discovering that the benefits of the rehabilitation program, although generous in regard to training, provided meager subsistence allowances. And unlike MDTA, the rules did not allow the trainee to supplement the subsistence with additional earnings. The clientele of the Department of Vocational Rehabilitation had traditionally been persons who were not totally dependent on the subsistence allowances they received. The staff in the Adult Opportunity Center offices found that many of their clients who participated in the vocational rehabilitation program dropped out because the subsistence allowance was simply too low to allow a person to continue in a sustained training program.

Thus, the interviewer already working in the ghetto, especially if he had experienced a multi-agency operation, was most skeptical about the value of the State Service Center program to the poor when it was proposed. He knew that the Service Centers would not provide any additional outlets or resources for him. He knew that no matter how many different agencies and how much staff and space were provided, most individuals came into the office looking for a job and would eventually be referred to *his* desk. And no matter how well touted as a one-stop service, no matter how grand the language, the office would still have the same jobs coming over the same teletype, the same number of training slots and types of training programs, the same difficulty with community resources. The interviewer also knew that no matter by what name the agency was called, the services he personally had provided would not be bettered because they were provided under another guise. He had not found it particularly difficult to telephone a vocational rehabilitation officer in his office and arrange an appointment for a client when that resource was indicated — which was rather rare. All the State Service Center program meant to the employment interviewer was that he would now be able to walk across the room to the vocational rehabilitation counselor instead of making the telephone call. The entire program, when brought down to the daily grind as he knew it, appeared to add zero to zero. If anything, it would lose the particular value that comes from operating a small installation under a single agency. At least there the interviewer had only one kind of form to worry about, and he wasn't the subject of two bureaucratic structures hammering at him and pulling him in opposite directions.

The Service Center programs did go into effect, although the number of centers was considerably reduced from the original plan. In San Francisco the center was housed for an extended time in makeshift offices but eventually moved into a converted grocery store in the heart of the ghetto. The center was heavily staffed with employment service personnel and had a total staff of approximately eighty. This complex operation was located only four blocks from the employment service's Adult Opportunity Center, with its small staff operating out of an old Victorian house. It soon became evident that the two offices were duplicating clients and orders. At first, an attempt was made to maintain the Adult Opportunity Center to provide special programs, workshops, and tutoring, but the bureaucracy could not justify the staffing of two separate components within four blocks of one another. In 1970, the rental lease expired on the old Victorian house, and the Adult Opportunity Center was closed. Three remaining Adult Opportunity Center offices were eventually converted into Human Resources Development Centers.

The State Service Center program had some important influences on the employment service. The main body of administrators and policy makers were drawn from other state agencies such as the Department of Vocational Rehabilitation and the Department of Corrections and Social Welfare. Most of the center management staff, as well as state administrators, were members of minority groups. This was the first real infusion of top minority administrators into the manpower field. The most characteristic concept of service that was brought into the employment area by the influx of new administrators — the caseload model — sprang from the past experiences of these new administrators and was superimposed on the manpower situation. Elaborate forms were designed, and an extensive training program was instituted in order to develop the ability of staff to do and record casework. Interviewers began describing their collective job seekers as the "case load."

Whether or not casework is a valid model in other fields, one glaring difference between manpower and other services is immediately evident. The "glue" that binds a parole officer to a parolee, a vocational rehabilitation counselor to a client, a welfare social worker to a welfare recipient, a doctor to a patient, and a lawyer to a defendant is power — the power to give or withhold. Parole agents have the power to return a man to prison. Social workers can approve or disapprove a person's welfare support. A vocational rehabilitation counselor has at his personal command considerable sums of money to be paid to — or withheld from — doctors, training institutions, and individuals. The contract between donor and recipient, be it money, school, or freedom, is fairly clear no matter how gently it is presented. The donor has the power to alter the recipient's life, to do him good or ill.

An interviewer in a manpower center has no money, no power, and no skills or knowledge potent enough to manipulate the external world. No legal mandate or income support tie most job seekers to the agency. A man coming in to look for work hardly regarded himself as a "case." And since he didn't know he was a "case," he ceased being one when he disappeared into his own life. The entire elaborate case system was wholly internal. Cases were shifted, teams were formed, new cases were added, and old ones were purged as inactive. Most cases became inactive not because of the services rendered but because the individuals disappeared. Nobody told them that they were supposed to behave like cases. But the casework concept, with its ego-satisfying paraphernalia and verbiage, its excess of paper work, its trappings of a personalized service, pervaded the entire agency. It was all form and no content.

The State Service Center program did make one tremendously significant contribution, which eventually was felt in every local office in northern California. The Service Center in the "Western Addition" area of San Francisco opened up the jobs to public scrutiny. It established the first Job Information Center within its offices, staffed with workers who circulated among the job seekers, offered advice and assistance, and made the appropriate job referrals. The center was attractively designed and executed. All of the job listings were hung on the wall, with the employers' names and addressed obscured. The effect of the Job Information Center was jolting to both the ghetto users and the agency. The center area was always crowded and in use. Many employees from other offices of the agency came to visit the center and watch the operation. The manager reported an immediate jump in the placement count, despite the persistently poor job orders that graced the walls. The Service Center was able to do openly what the Adult Opportunity Center in the Western Addition could only do surreptitiously, because the Service Center manager was not part of the employment security bureaucracy; he was employed by the State Service Center itself.

Without a doubt, one reason the Job Information Center was able to show an improved performance was that it broke the counter barrier. The operations which took place behind the counter were no longer mysterious, the job list was available for all to see, and employment service workers circulated freely among the job seekers.

But that important "breakthrough" at the Job Information Center had its roots in earlier ghetto experiences. It was preceded by events at the Adult Opportunity Center just a few blocks away, where the counter barrier was not only symbolically bridged but the physical structure of the counter itself was eliminated. The "counter" point of the Adult Opportunity Center in 1966 became not just a view from the counter but a counter view in the sense that it was new and different and exciting.

The Employment Service in the Ghetto

The Adult Opportunity Center project in San Francisco was proposed by the staff of the northern California coastal area office and funded in 1965 by an experimental and demonstration grant under the Manpower Development and Training Act. There were many cities in the country where the employment service placed staff members into already existing offices in poverty areas which were operated by the local antipoverty agency or other such entities. In Oakland, for instance, the Adult Opportunity Centers were jointly administered by the employment service and the city's antipoverty agency. But the San Francisco project was unique because the employment service itself was funded to place its own offices into that highly visible and exposed position. Although cooperative agreements were established with San Francisco's antipoverty installations in each of the city's four target areas, the employment service itself was solely and fully responsible for the centers. It shared that responsibility with no other agency.

The problems of the disadvantaged community — particularly its male population — were worsened in San Francisco by the changing economy of the city. Never an industrial center, San Francisco had been steadily losing its blue-collar jobs to the surrounding communities as factories and warehouses moved outside the city. The city had become primarily a financial, commercial, and government center. The blue-collar work that did exist was largely controlled by trade unions that were among the strongest in the country. With the exception of the longshoremen, warehousemen, and lower skill construction unions — which have high ratios of black members — the low-paying, low-status, high-turnover jobs in the service occupations were the major source of work for the unskilled or semiskilled men of the minority community. Women with clerical or medical aide skills were more easily absorbed into financial and commercial institutions.

The Adult Opportunity Center project was designed to place employment services into four communities: two predominantly black, one in a Spanish-speaking area, and one in Chinatown. The project designated unemployed, unskilled males as the primary target population. It must be remembered that the emphasis on males reflected the popular wisdom of the times. In both academic and civil rights circles the theory was being promulgated that the road to full integration could best be traveled by strengthening the economic position of the family "head" in the black community. This was interpreted as strengthening the position of the black male relative to the black woman. It is unlikely that either the theory or the practice would be allowed to go unchallenged today. In order to ensure that the offices would not be diverted from the target population, Adult Opportunity Centers were instructed not to accept or handle domestic job orders or applicants seeking only domestic work. Skilled, easily placed individuals were to be referred to the appropriate downtown offices. It was understood that interviewers in those offices accustomed to dealing with clerical and professional occupations or with domestic work would provide such skilled applicants with better service. The design of the project did not spell out methodology; it simply posed the goal of bringing traditional employment services to the disadvantaged with attention to the new definitions for services which were then emerging.

The office to be described was located in one of the black communities known as the Western Addition. It was housed on two levels of a three-story Victorian house. The big dining room adjoining the kitchen became the focal point for both clientele and staff. It was there, around two large tables in the center of the room — with the ever-present coffee urn — that groups of unemployed black men sat with members of the staff four nights a week for three and a half years in an effort to hassle out their relationship to the work world. Called "workshops" by the staff, but known widely in the ghetto as "meetings," some 2,500 men — and occasionally women — confronted the white bureaucracy, learned from it, and taught it.

It was around those tables that the staff itself designed programs, argued positions, and confronted the inevitable disagreements. From that nerve center came a volunteer adult tutorial program involving eighty volunteer tutors, an unfunded computer operator training program considered one of the most successful in the country, and myriad innovations, techniques, and services that were inconceivable in a normal employment service operation. Some of these were effective; some failed.

The process by which the office shifted away from the traditional mold and evolved new approaches is as important as the programs that developed.

To staff the Adult Opportunity Centers, administrators asked the entire employment service staff for those who would be willing to transfer voluntarily, with particular emphasis on the recruitment of Spanish-speaking, Chinese, and black staff. However, most of the Adult Opportunity Center staff, when finally selected, consisted of new, young employees of the department who had just completed their official training and had very little experience in any employment service office. A number were "employment community workers," a California State classification that permitted the agency to recruit and hire black and chicano men and women from poverty communities.

Administratively, all four Adult Opportunity Centers were considered as a single local office with a single manager, but each of the installations had its own branch manager. For that reason, training of staff, allocation of MDTA slots, and other personnel and administrative processes were carried on centrally for all four installations.

The training of the newly assigned staff was developed and conducted independently from the area training center and reflected the changed emphasis nationally. The 35 persons initially hired to man the four centers were subject to a concentrated, one-week effort which included the technique of sending trainees out to simulate the job search and thus experience what happened to clients on the other side of the counter. The training provided heavy emphasis on the advocacy role, on ghetto culture, and on problems of the disadvantaged.

The Western Addition Adult Opportunity Center opened its door in May of 1965 with a staff of eight. Although the racial composition of the staff shifted at various times in the ensuing years, about half were members of minority groups. At least two regular staff members were recruited from the local population. Over the next four years, the staff consisted at most of twelve persons, but it dropped to as low as six. The opening of the office was accompanied by some fanfare and newspaper announcements, and there was an immediate flow of traffic.

During the planning stages the one issue around which everyone within the agency seemed to unite was that the office should be untraditional in outside and inside appearances. The stream of suggestions included: "No counters," "more homey," "some gay colors," "some warmth," "can't we get rid of these grey metal desks?," "magazines to read," "pictures on the wall," "small." The comments showed a common effort to send out this message with the first impact: "We aren't that impersonal, insulting monolith you have known. We're real human beings, and we know you are too."

The enthusiasm that greeted the effort, the array of curtains, plants, vases, and other decorative and useful items brought by staff members revealed a wish to ease the discomfort of the job seekers in this new situation. But it revealed something else also. Those members of the staff who had experienced the traditional office clearly demonstrated how oppressive the paraphernalia symbolized by the counter was to them and how much they themselves were imprisoned by it. They sought freedom to be themselves as well as to relieve the ghetto residents of the frustrations usually associated with their contact with the agency.

The old Victorian house reflected this. There were *no* counters. The walls were decorated with pictures of cultural and racial heroes, current posters, and some labor market information. Interviewers' desks were in an area that extended without any barrier from the waiting area. A staff member or greeter, went *to* the people and ascertained their needs.

When the Adult Opportunity Center opened for business, applicants poured in. They were greeted by a relatively inexperienced staff, few of whom had ever developed a familiarity with any group of employers or knew anthing about the city or jobs. But they were eager to help. They took work applications and coded them. The only tools the interviewers were given by the agency were blank job order forms, work applications, manuals, and the *Dictionary of Occupational Titles.*

And there it stopped. There were no manpower training slots available at that point. Even worse, there was not a single job order.

An administrative decision had been made to withhold from the Adult Opportunity Centers the open orders obtained in the regular offices. This decision was a result of resistance by the downtown agency offices, which were understandably concerned about maintaining good relationships with employers. Thus, not even the meager resources of the agency were initially shared. Had there been a trickle of jobs sent over, the true paucity of the agency's resources for the disadvantaged might not have surfaced so quickly. But the realities were painfully clear: an office, a staff, people coming through the door, paper work — and not one job order. The much touted manpower services being offered to ghetto residents were these: an inexperienced staff checking help-wanted ads in the newspapers, calling strange employers from the yellow pages to solicit jobs, and becoming overnight social workers in an attempt to grapple with major problems generated by centuries of racial injustice.

It was out of this total frustration that the evening workshops for unemployed men developed, the meetings which became the hallmark of the office. The staff and supervisor were outraged at their impotency and reacted with a resolve that they would not be a party to perpetrating fraud on the ghetto residents. The office sought ways to tell the truth about "employment services" and to alert the local populace against placing reliance on help from such meager resources. The staff searched for ways to help clients use their own resources.

The first attempt came just two weeks after the office was opened. Applicants were asked to return after working hours for a discussion. The effect of "leveling" with those who showed up that night — "We want you to know the truth; we haven't any jobs!" — and the ensuing discussion was so unexpected, heartwarming, and productive that the office resolved then and there to continue the evening meetings. Techniques were refined, workshop leadership was developed, and schedules were adjusted to ensure staff coverage for day and evening "shifts." The workshops became the major source of information and inspiration for the staff, the kernel of office activities. Eventually, when the word spread, they were the object of innumerable VIP "visits" and the pride of the agency.

The workshops were an unexpected benefit, born of utter frustration because there were no job orders. But they continued long after the initial administrative decision was reversed to allow the Adult Opportunity Centers access by teletype to all employments service job orders. The office ran an outreach employment office in the daytime and group work at night.

It might be useful to recall the placement process as described in the traditional office, circa 1962, and examine each element as it applied to an office where the applicant population was low-skill and often long-term unemployed. It should be stated at the outset that although the staff consisted of employment security officers, employment community workers, counselors, supervisor, and clerks, all functions quickly fused and lost distinction. The clerk was taught to assist a man to fill out his application card; a supervisor was apt to be interviewing; interviewers counseled; employment community workers did placement work; and counselors acted as receptionists.

Although the office went through considerable changes during its four-year existence, the traditional functions and work loads were generally divided along the following lines. Each new applicant was given a work application card and advised to wait for a placement interviewer. This usually meant that the next free interviewer would take him. The interviewer who took the application retained the responsibility for the man. (The office functioned on a rudimentary case load basis to the degree that it meant personal responsibility for a group of applicants.) One interviewer performed all functions for the applicant, from the completion to the follow-up. The interviewer kept his own applicant file box on his desk, and he had full responsibility for the individuals in that file. He scanned his own file to select applicants for available jobs, MDTA slots, apprenticeship openings, New Career slots, non-funded training courses, tutoring help, or any other jobs or programs either received by or developed by the office. The intake documents — work applications — were decentralized to each interviewer. The outlet documents — job orders on training and educational opportunity information — were centralized.

Because of the multitude of problems facing applicants, an informal team concept emerged, with considerable consultation and division of specialty. The effectiveness of this teamwork can be attributed partially to the fact that the staff was small. Staff members called for help from one another openly and in the presence of the applicant. No attempt was made to appear all-knowing. Admissions of uncertainty or the lack of resources or jobs were openly made. One interviewer developed a great fund of "hustle" information — where to get free bus tickets, how to get a hungry man a meal and a place to sleep. Another developed a relationship with an unusually receptive group of employers at the airport and was able to develop jobs. The specialties were shared as the need arose.

The entire staff always invited the applicants to attend the evening workshops.

Interviewers quickly found that the completion of a regular work application had no significance whatsoever in the office. Most applicants fell within a narrow and often interchangeable range of unskilled occupations, so the coding was of little help. Work histories were spotty and yielded little information of placement value. File search was unproductive because the applicants frequently changed addresses; few had stable home telephones; and even when an applicant's home could be reached, language or personal problems often cropped up. The application card was

not only a useless tool for placement on a job, it was equally in-
effective as a device for selecting MDTA trainees. It was even
inadequate for internal statistical or evaluative purposes, since it
did not ask for the kind of personal data that described the range
of problems requiring attention — such pertinent eligibility factors
as arrest records, income, and so on. The uselessness of the work
application as it stood prompted all of the Adult Opportunity Centers to develop supplementary forms. In the Western Addition it
was determined that whenever an application was taken, a duplicate copy would be prepared and handed to the applicant. The
process of taking a complete standard work application on every
person proved to be a dismaying waste of time and of little value.

The work applications did serve one purpose, however ob-
lique. The quality of the self-completing forms was so poor that
it called the staff's attention to the need to develop techniques for
teaching people how to fill out a competitive application card
when looking for work. That teaching process became one of the
concerns of the evening workshops. Job seekers working together
completed an application card during the workshops. These were
typed and refined during the day by a clerk, in duplicate, one
copy being retained by the office and the other given to the applicant to use as a guideline when filling out employer's application
cards. It astonished the staff to discover that many men had deliberately avoided seeking work in bigger companies and in civil
service because they had been unable to confront elaborate work
applications. The model they took with them allowed them to
broaden their search.

The placement function consisted mostly of individual job
development, with interviewers cajoling, pleading, and sometimes
harassing employers into interviewing a client. Efforts were made
to negotiate with groups of employers to change their hiring standards. For example, the Adult Opportunity Center called a conference with hospital personnel in the city in an attempt to per-
suade them to view more sympathetically the absence of letters of
reference and to consider the differences between an arrest record
for smoking marijuana as against a conviction for "dealing."

The open job orders which came in on the teletype from the
two major downtown offices or which were phoned directly to the
Adult Opportunity Centers by employers could usually be handled

by the daily normal flow of traffic. There were few enough good jobs. Most job openings received or developed were in the service occupations. The discouraging reality of San Francisco's economic structure could not be manipulated by either staff or user. Since the selection process attempts to match the skills of the man to the skill requirements of the job, the lower the skill level, the less pertinent is the selection process. File search often took the form of mass mailing to selected groups of applicants in order to fill a mass order or to inform the registered applicants about a training program.

The entire counseling function, as practiced in the traditional office, fell apart in the ghetto. The criteria by which staff would normally refer an applicant to a counselor became ludicrous and inoperable. It was apparent that most of the job seekers suffered from a multiplicity of problems that transcended the mere problem of occupational choices. The traditional counseling clues selected those who were either new entrants on the labor market or needed help in selecting or changing their occupational goals. The bulk of the applicants in the ghetto had far less concern with occupational goals than with immediate employment and overcoming those obstacles that prevented them from getting a footing on the very first rung of almost any ladder.

Trained counselors found that the traditional skills and tools they had acquired were not only irrelevant, they were sometimes downright destructive. What might have been seen as professional decorum in a normal setting became professional arrogance and a "put down" in the ghetto. Many of the office's clients had been "counseled" to death. Employment counseling presupposes that the job seeker has alternatives from which to select a course of action. It is normally a slow process that involves an unfolding of the client in a series of interviews, tests, and discussions. Among the clients of the Western Addition office, there were realistic alternatives that ran the gamut from A to B (as Dorothy Parker once said in describing the performance of an actress with limited talent). The urgent demands of the landlord and the grocer left the client disinclined to enter into a leisurely exploration of his long-range potentials. The personal problems that emerged were totally beyond the scope of the counselor's training or the resources available from either the employment service or other agencies.

And what distressed some of the staff was that the counseling stance reinforced black apathy and dependency on more powerful figures. This was contrary to the goals of the workshops, which sought to mobilize the individual's own resources. The palpable inappropriateness and impotence of the one-to-one individual counseling situation with most applicants was one important reason for shifting the office focus so heavily in the direction of group activity — group counseling, group information giving, group selection processes, and group teaching. The staff came to depend on the peer group situation to provide that motivating, reality-testing, supportive jolt by which so many of the men were, in fact, moved to act in their own behalf.

All in all, the tools and functions that together had once comprised what was meant by the term "employment services" proved to be of minimal value to the job seeker and the interviewer in this new situation.

The most valuable of the traditional skills — knowledge of a particular occupation and the ability to negotiate knowledgeably and authoritatively with employers — were slowly developed by the relatively new staff. But the realities of the situation made those skills of secondary importance. What *did* have clear value to those who came to the office was the atmosphere of the office, the warmth of the staff, and the honesty of the information offered.

There was value in the willingness of an established bureaucracy to become visible and available in the ghetto, in the programs and activities that developed in response to the needs of the users, and to some degree, in the funded manpower training programs. For the staff, the experience was invaluable. They developed an entirely different knowledge and consciousness of the ghetto world, and in turn they transmitted this to others in the agency. They had the opportunity to test their own capacities, to develop skills, and to experience a growing trust in their own judgment. The manuals are somewhat symbolic of the change in emphasis; although the office had been provided with the inevitable set of manuals, they fell into complete disuse. The endless manual amendments were relegated to the wastebasket.

At the same time, new resources *were* provided by the government. A whole series of funded manpower training programs descended on the office. The programs offered occupational training in many forms, usually coupled with subsistence allowances to trainees. An office such as the one in Western Addition was notified of a project and provided with the ground rules and the number of slots to be filled. The office then set out to recruit its unemployed clientele to fill those training programs. In addition to regular institutional MDTA training classes and individual MDTA training slots, programs included New Careers, on-the-job training, and the Concentrated Employment Program. The responsibility of the office was to select the trainees, determine their eligibility, sign them up for the training, keep contact with them while they were in training, and place them on jobs when they finished.

There were innumerable pitfalls. The most serious, of course, were the limitations in the kinds of occupations for which it was possible to train, especially in San Francisco. Most programs were initially limited to a six-month period, which is hardly adequate for developing usable skills in individuals who have virtually no skills at all. Clerical training programs were easily filled and usually productive, as were those for licensed vocational nurses. But these were generally regarded as women's occupations. The clientele of the Western Addition office was mostly men. And the narrow range of training programs for janitors, welders, auto body men, and fry cooks was either not appropriate or uninviting for many of the clients.

Selection of trainees for any of the federally funded manpower programs was a far cry from what was envisioned in official documents. There was *never* enough lead time between the final approval of a training project and the starting date of the course. Interest cards from applicants were accepted and retained in the office files for months, but by the time programs became a reality, people were otherwise occupied, were lost, or couldn't be reached. With only a few days allowed to fill the allocated slots, interviewers found themselves reduced to grabbing anyone they could lay their hands on who was willing to go into training.

Even more fundamental, however, was the problem of criteria for selecting trainees. Eligibility for various manpower programs was determined by a mixture of criteria designed to reach a particular target group. They included such factors as length of unemployment, poverty level, position in the family, age, and residency in an economically depressed area. It often seemed to the interviewers that the elaborate combinations of criteria could more productively have been reduced to one meaningful criterion — the work history. Only the work history reflected and telegraphed the prognosis for successful training. However, the program criteria defined only different levels of desperation and alienation from the work world. Often eligibility for one program was in sharp conflict with eligibility for another. Further limiting the chance for successful selection was the continuous injunction against "creaming" the applicant supply for the most promising candidates. "Creaming" would have resulted in selections which tended to exclude people with extreme problems, such as extensive arrest records, poor work histories, and histories of mental problems.

Once eligibility was determined, no other criteria for selecting one candidate over another was ever established, with the exception of a basic education test for some programs. Since a person was to be trained to do what he had never done before, no other factors on the application card were either qualifying or disqualifying. What measure could the interviewer apply, what judgment could he summon, to select one poor person as against another equally poor person when the entire file was filled with poor persons? The old criteria for job selection were useless, and no new ones were provided other than eligibility by need. It was as if the disadvantaged were conceived of as a mass whose only distinguishable features were degree of poverty. Over and over, interviewers saw needful people who wanted training and who were regarded as appropriate choices, only to find that they didn't fit into the precise poverty pattern defined by that program. And just as often, the interviewers found themselves approving trainees for programs which were inappropriate and which didn't really interest the applicants. It was as if failure were built in. Selections tended to be poor risks. Inevitably, "program hustlers" permeated the training, and individuals were put into training programs merely because they were available and wanted the stipend.

It came to matter little whether the programs were good or bad. The combined number of training slots was so small, so insignificant when set against the available applicant supply, that the office staff found itself reluctant to tout the programs. For example, in an entire year, the Western Addition office might have had access to only 100 to 150 slots, which included all manner of discrete programs. With an active application file of two thousand at any given time, this represented help, however meager and questionable, for only 5 to 7 percent of the applicants. Nevertheless, the funded federal manpower programs did represent a tool, a resource.

There were many occasions, with many individuals, when the whole process actually worked and worked well, where staff could see significant changes taking place in the lives and aspirations of applicants because of one or another manpower training program. This was most frequently true of individual MDTA training slots, which allowed the training program to be designed for a particular individual's needs. This individual approach was most successful, although it did represent much more work for the interviewer.

From the viewpoint of a conscientious interviewer, it is possible to say that the entire experience of the employment service in the ghetto consisted of a series of exploded myths, lost innocences, romantic pitfalls. Despite remarkable successes, an increasing sense of powerlessness and a deepening awareness of the immensity and complexity of manpower problems came to the whole staff. Each new resource that came into the office carried its own promise and its own disappointments. For example, when the area office decision to withhold job orders from Adult Opportunity Centers was reversed and the downtown job orders appeared on the teletype, many of the interviewers who hadn't worked a placement desk in the downtown offices were elated until they realized how few usable jobs were being distributed to eight offices. It was as if the great machine whirled, buzzed, glittered, and then produced a toothpick.

But just as the office found ways to turn the application-taking process into a useful tool for the applicant, so it found ways to use job orders as a tool that transcended the original intent. One of the problems in the office was the limited labor market information available for the staff. If the staff was to motivate job seekers to use their own resources in the labor market, as it was determined to do, it became imperative that the staff have a working knowledge of the labor market and its operation.

The meager knowledge of the staff was serious enough. But the meager knowledge, the distortions, and the misconceptions of the users were amazing. The market they knew well was the "secondary" market — the extremely limited range of low-paying occupations. But they knew next to nothing about breaking out of those narrow confines. And since the office conceived of its role as something more than matching a man who had always been in and out of work as a dishwasher to yet another dishwashing job — since the office saw its mission as finding those cracks that would enable a man to break out of that cycle — information about those cracks and what might be on the other side of them became of crucial importance.

Picture, if you will, a staff member conducting a workshop of some ten men. Because the workshop was task oriented, it was the responsibility of the workshop leader to end the workshop by ensuring that every man who intended to look for a job could be assigned a place to go the following day with some practice in his approach, in his interview technique, and in completing an application card. The workshop process then required that the job seeker return the following evening and put his experiences before the group for analysis and mutual learning. Where to send a person, then, was a critical consideration for the workshop. It had to be a place where the man could at least walk through the door. Each evening, that grim moment came when the workshop leader floundered because he didn't know what places to assign. He didn't know enough about the San Francisco labor market, about employers, about unions, about hiring practices in various occupations, about what the job seeker would encounter, or about how to prepare him for that encounter.

This might have been understandable if the workshop leaders were all new and inexperienced. But the two most active leaders were experienced employees of the agency who had been working in the regular local offices for a number of years. They were as alert, as bright, and as well trained as anyone in the employment service. And yet they simply didn't know where to send applicants. They clearly reflected the agency's traditional "tunnel vision." In their panic these experienced interviewers began the search to learn more, to gather more information, and to develop new kinds of tools. The manager went to the research and statistics section of the agency, described the problem, and asked for help. Staff members from the research and statistics section were urged to attend the workshops and experience the problem themselves. They did — with telling results. They began to devise guides for the job search in various occupations in San Francisco. A rudimentary library was developed. One interviewer conceived the brilliant notion that inactive orders might be of value. He solicited inactive orders from all the other offices and filed them, not alphabetically as had been traditional, but by occupation. When the moment came in the workshop to talk about where to go, the workshop leader had a whole range of places to suggest. The inactive order file became the richest source of information available. It contained the names of hundreds of companies which had had, at one time or another in the preceding few years, an opening for people with particular skills. Each job order described the special characteristics of the job, the hiring practices of the company, the pay, the shifts, the need for references, the willingness to train. Not only did that file serve the workshop leaders, it also served interviewers as a source of information in developing jobs for individuals. Its obvious value influenced subsequent developments in the agency.

The disappointments that attended the actual appearance of the job orders prompted other experimentation. The office was profoundly committed to the elimination of any agency "games" with the clientele, and one of the saddest games of all was the "hidden order syndrome." That was the game of thumbing through the jobs in the order box, hiding the demand list, but under no circumstances allowing the applicant to see them. Contrary to all the manuals — and even in violation of the law — the office developed the practice of allowing applicants to *see* the open orders. During the workshops the active orders would be tossed on the table for the men to read. It was plain that reading the orders had a great teaching and motivating impact. Few applicants chose to pursue jobs for which they were not qualified. Indeed, the reverse was true. The persons who came to that office tended strongly to underrate themselves, to passively accept their positions. In fact, it was that very passivity and inertia that the office was doing battle with.

During the day applicants could see the teletype, watch the job orders being torn off, and see what happened to them. They knew the office was hiding nothing. The scarcity of appropriate and decent jobs also helped applicants realize that they would have to motivate themselves to find work, that the powerful agency really consisted of some nice people with few jobs. It was not really possible to develop a dependency on such an agency.

At that point in time, the experiment with opening up the jobs was daring and clandestine. Since then, the Job Information Centers in all the offices in northern California and the computerized Job Banks in offices across the nation have served somewhat the same purpose.

Although MDTA slots were eagerly awaited by both staff and clients, the program soon raised more questions than it answered. Both staff and clients wondered about the commitment and competency of adult education programs in the area. Community restraints that prevented training in certain occupations became painfully obvious. The validity and the appropriateness of MDTA selection guidelines were openly questioned, as were the motives of many trainees under the program. But perhaps the most serious question was whether or not the job market was really ready to accept "graduates" from MDTA programs.

More than any other national manpower program, the New Careers program appealed to the disadvantaged. They saw the program as a recognition that they had inherent capabilities which had heretofore been untapped. They saw it as a way out of their entrapment in the secondary labor market. Publicity and word-of-mouth brought hundreds of competitors for New Career slots. But disillusionment followed for both staff and applicants when the low wage rates and the small number of available slots were announced. In its whole existence, the Western Addition office had access to a total of no more than 25 New Careers openings.

Some programs were unqualified successes, at least from the point of view of the ghetto office. A successful program could be described as one which promises something that is strongly desired, and then fulfills its promise. For example, immediately after the racial riots in Hunters Point, the mayor's office established an emergency job center. When hundreds of federal jobs were suddenly made available, the Adult Opportunity Center joyfully recruited from the swarms of people who responded to the newspaper publicity. The jobs actually existed. The U. S. Postal Service, for instance, waived entrance tests on the condition that those who would continue to work beyond a year would be required to pass the test within that year. The test would be offered three times during the year. Because the Adult Opportunity Center staff was intimately aware of the problems which that population had regarding test taking, it sought to alert the various agencies to the need for a tutorial program for the new post office employees. The center managers pleaded with school officials to begin a teaching program. But the school department was unwilling to consider the proposal until such a program could be fully funded. When time for the first test drew near, representatives from the post office called the center for advice. Clients, too, called to ask for help. There was no place to send them. Responding to this emergency, the four center managers developed a test-taking teaching program, each session of which was to last approximately twelve hours. The program was to run for two weeks in order to absorb as many new employees as possible. Training material was developed. Volunteer tutors were recruited from the community and trained. Staff members volunteered their time. Literally hundreds of individuals participated. And although the hastily prepared tutoring did not suceed in getting the bulk of the new post office employees through the test successfully, it did help some, and it did serve to point out the need. Months later, after MDTA funding, the local schools instituted a test preparation course.

The continuing tutorial program established by the office and continued even after the office closed could be considered a successful effort. It provided something that was wanted, and it fulfilled its promises. It developed because the men in the workshops demanded it. The nightly discussions revealed to them how often their own personal experiences were duplicated; they didn't get jobs because they didn't pass tests. And they began to demand that the office show some response to that need, insisting that they were "turned off by the schools." With a staff of ten and with an office already open some fourteen hours a day, it seemed an impossible demand. Staff members solicited their friends. One trained teacher was found who volunteered her time to develop a program, to obtain materials, and to recruit other volunteers. In time, the agency found a way to put her on a part-time payroll.

The tutorial program grew in size, stature, and techniques. At least eighty volunteers were trained, and well over a thousand persons participated as learners at various points. The tutorial program took on many tasks and forms. It not only provided one-to-one tutoring in basic education, but it extended its service to the other Adult Opportunity Centers with language tutoring. It also developed techniques for preparing applicants for the general education development (GED) test, and it ran group teaching programs to underpin MDTA courses. For example, several women were having difficulty in their licensed vocational nurse course. The tutorial program was called upon to deal with the problem, and a doctor was found to volunteer his help at night. Groups were coached in order to prepare for specific employment tests. Employers, such as the airlines, called on the tutorial program to prepare minority employees for their upgrading examinations.

Most tutoring took place in the evening. The Western Addition Center often looked like a community center in the evening, with every nook and corner occupied by people involved in some kind of activity — workshops, tutoring, or reading. The drinking of coffee never ended, and the supply — donated by local merchants — never gave out.

Perhaps educators would have serious doubts about whether or not the tutorial program was of great value from an educational standpoint. There is no way of knowing how much progress students actually made, although many did indeed pass the GED, get through the MDTA course, and pass the employers' tests. It would obviously be scientifically invalid to insist that it wouldn't have happened without the tutoring, but one thing was certain: Clients were coming back, night after night — some for years. These were individuals who would never have gone to the regular adult education courses. And a great number were inspired enough — and had their fears reduced enough — to actually enroll in adult education as a direct result of their tutorial experience. In time, the agency assigned two full-time workers to run the program, and it continued long after the Western Addition office was closed. It was the only adult volunteer program in the city that survived for an extended period.

While some of the MDTA training programs were partially successful, the most successful training program was one which was developed by the Adult Opportunity Center itself.

It began one night during a workshop when a man came and announced that he was the data processing manager of a major firm in San Francisco. He had heard of the workshops and had come to offer his services because he felt he could train some of the participants to be computer programmers. After much discussion, he decided to go to IBM for help with written material.

The IBM educational center, by coincidence, was searching for an appropriate ghetto training program because money had been allocated nationally for that purpose. The data processing manager arranged a meeting between the manager of the Western Addition Adult Opportunity Center and the direction of the IBM Educational Center. It didn't take long to determine that the programming field was too diffiicult because it required a college degree for entry. Instead, IBM offered to design a special concentrated course for computer operators.

Without federal or state funds, the Adult Opportunity Center undertook the partnership.

Over a period of a year and a half, six courses were conducted with an average of 22 trainees to a class. Although the course material was difficult and demanding, the retention rate was 90 percent. Over 600 persons participated in the group selection process, approximately 120 for each course. Of the 110 or so who completed the training and received their IBM certificates, 85 percent were placed in the data processing field on jobs that paid approximately 25 percent more than had been anticipated by the office when it announced the course. Given the average 50 percent dropout rate of funded MDTA programs and 50 percent placement rates for those who graduate, the results of the computer operator training program were nothing short of phenomenal.

The janitor *did* become a computer operator, and his life *did* change.

In order to avoid the traps of eligibility mixes and poverty criteria, the office refused to seek or accept federal funding. Operating on the principle that the fact of being employed or unemployed for the moment was of little significance in the ghetto view of the nature of most jobs, the office designed the program for a different target group. The criteria established called for the staff to seek out those persons, employed or unemployed, who were frozen into unskilled occupations and had no obvious alternatives available. In addition to that, a person had to be trainable, he had to be strongly motivated, and he had to convince the workshop group that his commitment was a serious one. Intuitively, the staff was searching for a way to move people from the secondary labor market into more satisfying primary jobs. Only in this way could the office hope to make significant changes in the lives of the people who sought change.

IBM undertook to design the training, to provide instructors, to make available the training facilities at the educational center, and most important of all, to provide "hands-on" machine time to the trainees. Of course, IBM had access to this machine time to a far greater degree than expensive private schools. The company also offered to prepare certificates of graduation and to provide their computer operator selection test, which was geared for a pass mark of 25. With some trepidation, IBM representatives agreed to accept those who achieved a mark of 16 or better.

Except for the training component, it was determined that the Western Addition Adult Opportunity Center staff would have the responsibility of designing every aspect of the program. This was to include recruiting and selecting trainees, assisting trainees while they were in the course, developing job openings, teaching trainees how to conduct an interview in the data processing field, placing the graduates in jobs, and continuing contact with them after placement. Recruitment was extended to all four Adult Opportunity Centers, the antipoverty offices, and the regular downtown offices.

Before beginning, the staff, with the help of the research and statistics section, did a thorough survey of data processing employers in order to be familiar with possibilities in the field, wage rates, upward mobility, entrance requirements, and pitfalls. The office was determined to be in a position to give an absolutely unglorified, factual picture to the potential trainees so they could make decisions based on real knowledge.

Because the program was unfunded and would therefore offer no stipend, it was essential that the office develop a selection method that tapped into the motives and goals of the competing applicants. Since the classes would include employed individuals, the training was designed for a twenty-hour week — four nights from six to nine and all day Saturday — to run approximately five weeks. Every single training session was critical, and the trainees were required to commit themselves to a very heavy, difficult and sustained effort. It was understood by the trainees that three absences would wash them out of the program, since it would be impossible for the instructor to make up that much of a lag.

The goal of the office was to select a class of trainees which allowed the office a reasonable chance to place the graduates on jobs. It was also the goal of the office to avoid the "creaming" process as much as possible. The ideal class, then, could not consist of twenty trainees with felony convictions, since that presented impossible placement odds for financial institutions. On the other hand, at least a few trainees should be selected despite the fact that they had felony convictions on their records. The program could absorb a few fifty-year-olds in an essentially youthful industry, but not twenty of them. It could ask the IBM trainer to cope with a few persons with language difficulties, but not twenty. As with the make-or-break test score, it sought to establish a class that tilted on the edge of the impossible but still allowed some hope of success for each individual, for the program itself, and for both the IBM trainer and the Adult Opportunity Center staff.

The selection process was vital to the program. In an article written by IBM officials, which appeared in a national computer magazine, the program was described in glowing terms. The article declared it to be the most successful of the many programs IBM ran for the disadvantaged throughout the country, and it attributed the success of the program to the innovative methods used in the selection process.

All selection was done in groups of approximately ten persons in two consecutive nights. The first night was devoted to giving information about the data processing field, the training course, and the kinds of jobs and wage rates that might become available. No one was allowed to apply at that point, because it was deemed important that those present first give serious consideration to their availability and the views of their families regarding participation in such a program. Those who continued to be interested as the evening ended were invited to return the next night. About

30 percent screened themselves out. Those who returned were told exactly what the selection criteria were. The group participated in the application process and in more personal discussions of their own particular qualifications, interests, and motivations. When the group heard from one man that he was 21 years old, was without family, had access to the GI Bill . . . and from the next that he had a wife and three children, had worked only as a janitor, and had been unable to break out of that position . . . the process of selection became much less secretive and accusatory. Every person there knew which of the two men should be selected, and some screened themselves out at that point.

Problems of drinking, drug use, convictions, old age, and the failure to complete previous training programs came into discussion. For those who chose to continue in the process of selection, the IBM computer operator test was scheduled. It was taken by all the remaining contenders together. It was made clear that the selections would not be based on the highest test score, only on the magical grade of 16, which would at least determine whether one's reading, reasoning, and computing abilities were adequate to absorb the training. Everyone was invited to return after the scores were in, if he wished, to participate in the staff discussion when the final selections were made. It was explained that the voting would be limited to the staff, because they were the only ones who saw *all* the contenders in all the groups, but any contender was welcome to come and argue his case.

And argue they did. The final selection always took place only a few days before the class was scheduled to start. It is safe to say that not one person who participated in the process ever wondered why he wasn't selected or what secret flaw he had that made him unacceptable. He knew exactly what the standards were, who his competitors were, and what influenced the decisions. Inevitably, the man who was selected had sat next to others who had been just as eager to enter the program and yet couldn't be absorbed. That the sense of inner commitment of those who were selected was strengthened by this we can infer from the unusual records which followed — in attendance, in promptness, and in headcracking efforts over the books.

Perhaps it might add another dimension to describe the first night of the first class. The success of the program hinged strongly on that scene. The IBM building is located far from the ghetto, in the very heart of San Francisco's financial district. Since the class started at six — after the building was closed — a uniformed doorman unlocked the door and ushered the men into the carpeted, plush foyer where they signed the building ledger. The doorman knew about the program, greeted the men, and directed them to the regular IBM training classroom. Outside the classroom stood an array of impressive data processing equipment. The classroom itself was airy, bright, and carpeted. In front of each chair on the long tables, a group of books, a leather-bound notebook, and pencils had been placed. And at each seat was a metal nameplate with the trainee's name on it. The staff members who were present watched the faces of the men as they found their own nameplates and listened to the trainer begin the class with: "Gentlemen, my name is . . . ." The moment was portentous and moving.

There was nothing second class or casual about the program, and the men knew it. From the moment they sat down, they knew they were privy to a serious effort on the part of the agency and a major "establishment" company. It called for an equal effort on the part of the trainees, which came forth so overwhelmingly as to amaze the trainer. Over the ensuing six series of classes, some fifty programmers and systems analysts who worked for IBM volunteered their time in the evening to assist the trainer, especially with the machine time. IBM also organized an impressive graduation ceremony for the first class, involving television, certificate awards, and speeches. And although it all may have served IBM's public relations needs, it also served the needs of the class when they had their efforts publicly acknowledged and lauded.

Job development in the computer operator training program also took some interesting turns. The first employer to hire a graduate was so impressed that he, along with several sympathetic data processing managers, solicited other employers for jobs. In a sense, some employers became extensions of the Adult Opportunity Center staff. They made speeches at meetings of data processing managers, arranged interviews for staff members, and pushed the program whenever possible.

Since the program did not exclude employed persons, companies were solicited which were employing trainees in janitorial or unskilled positions or had done so in the past. The City of San

Francisco, for example, arranged to transfer two city janitors who were graduates of the program into its data processing unit. One man who had barely made the required 16 marks on the test was so successful on the new job that he was subsequently sent back to IBM by the city for additional higher level training. A fifty-year-old man who had not held a job for ten years and whose arrest record was appalling went to work for an insurance company. One year later, he was the night supervisor. The entire program was studded with similar success stories.

About six months after he began work with the city data processing department, the former janitor dropped in to the center office. To a few staff members standing around at the close of the day, he said: "I went to a party last Saturday night. Someone asked me what I did for a living. Can you imagine, I didn't have to say 'janitor' any more. I said, 'I'm in data processing.' I sure felt good, and you should have seen how proud my wife was."

When he left, someone said, "There's not enough money in the world to pay me for how that made me feel."

When the second class began, ten members of the first class, who were by this time employed, made it their business to come to the evening classes and provide tutoring services to the new group of trainees.

It didn't take long for the residents of the ghetto to learn about the IBM program and its successes. Each new class brought more applicants. By the time the sixth class came along, jobs were becoming harder and harder to find. Thus, despite the desire of IBM to continue the program, despite pressure from many ghetto residents, and against the wishes of the agency, the Adult Opportunity Center made the decision to terminate the training. It was clear that the field was saturated, since the market was, at best, a limited one. The office was determined to train for jobs only when they realistically existed.

There were many lessons to be learned from the IBM computer training experiences, lessons about criteria for eligibility and the selection process. But it would be unfair not to add that a good part of the success of that program hinged on the fact that computer operations was a glamour occupation and IBM was a glamour company in the eyes of the ghetto residents. Those conditions do not always exist in every situation.

The Western Addition office of the Adult Opportunity Center was closed in late 1969, primarily because the State Service Center program, described earlier, had come into being. A State Service Center was established within four blocks of the Adult Opportunity Center. It was a huge, heavily staffed, multi-service office which included a large contingent of employment service staff. It became evident in time that the agency could not afford to staff both offices; neither was there any way to justify what appeared to be a duplication of services. The abandonment of the office was probably necessary from the agency viewpoint, but it was a loss to its users.

What did it accomplish? What can be learned from the experience? Did it succeed in its mission?

Imagine for a moment that the ghetto was a circumscribed area in 1965, inside which were an arbitrary number of individuals who were poor, disadvantaged, unemployed, underemployed, and in need of services. For the sake of clarity, assume that a thousand such individuals were counted in that area. A program came into the area, and by fair means and foul successfully moved four hundred of that thousand into another category. They were no longer poor, unemployed, and disadvantaged. The process took four years. But during that four years, a number of other things were happening. An undetermined number of young persons dropped out of school. Drugs became a national epidemic. New residents — most with problems — moved into the area. Migration from the south continued to send the unskilled into the area. A cynical decision in Washington to increase unemployment in order to fight inflation threw an indeterminate number of people into the area. The slowdown in the war and in defense spending tossed more people in. If an evaluator looked at the ghetto seven years later he would say: "My God, there are now fourteen hundred people in the area: The programs were a total failure."

If the manpower effort of the 1960s was seen as a means of solving major social and economic dislocations, then inevitably the Adult Opportunity Center effort was indeed a failure. If the effort was seen as a means of helping some human beings, then those four hundred individuals whose lives were changed could declare the program a success.

There are other points that should be made. One great value of putting an office in a poverty community is the knowledge that was gained about a whole host of client problems, knowledge that would have been diffused and would have gone unrecognized in a centralized, bureaucratic office. Unsuspected obstacles standing between a man and a job were continuously revealed. Who could have imagined, for example, that one of the big problems would be that applicants had no telephone number to leave with an employer when applying for work? The center office responded by offering a free telephone message service. Job seekers were often without letters of reference, birth certificates, or any of the paraphernalia necessary for the job hunt — and they didn't know how to get such items. The office clerk responded by devising form letters and offering a stenographic service to the clients. Men couldn't look for work because they had no bus fare. One interviewer started a campaign to get free tickets from the bus company, and still another interviewer ran an early morning bus service with his car. Some jobs required a driver's license, but if the job seeker didn't have three dollars or a car in which to take the test, he had no chance for the job. Interviewers loaned their own cars for the driving test and scrounged the license fee. Many applicants had appearance problems — poor clothes or no money for a haircut. An interviewer arranged for a student barber to come in. Another interviewer solicited clothes, and the office had a used clothes room. Someone else scrounged shaving equipment, to be kept in the office.

The effect of all these experiences on the higher echelon administrators in the area office was limited but evident. The prevalence of language problems encountered by the interviewers in the other Adult Opportunity Center offices prompted the coastal area staff to ask for and get funding from MDTA for language training. The failure of large numbers of applicants to pass California's sixth grade achievement test caused administrators to insist that remedial education be incorporated into the MDTA program.

But the learning — the reflections from the ghetto upward — apparently didn't get much beyond the coastal area, even though state and federal officials came, viewed, cheered, and sometimes recommended emulation. Perception was affected, but not action. The office was viewed as "our" success when Washington or Sacramento officials came. The dispassionate inquiry into what was learned about the population of the ghetto from listening to two thousand men pour their souls on that table was never undertaken. No mechanism existed for that. The experiences garnered from the Adult Opportunity Centers or any other such exposure in the country appears to have had no significant effect on the designers of new manpower programs and delivery systems intended for that target population. In fact, as programs proliferated they seemed to get further and further away from ghetto office realities. Nor is there any evidence that there was an interest by policy makers in learning what elements were present in the "successful" office that created the difference, that made the office "tick." No one really looked to the removal of all the air-poisoning agency devices as a possible explanation. No one thought to look at honesty as a factor.

In reexamining that interlude, evidence is ample that the main reason it was possible for that particular Adult Opportunity Center to try original and daring approaches was the loosened bureaucratic structure — the crack that appeared in the wall of the monolith, both nationally and locally. The area office, itself at a loss for answers and burdened with an ever-increasing overlay of federal manpower programs to administer, tended to give the center a free hand. The center staff complained that they were given very little help by the area staff, but correspondingly there was very little interference.

The lower echelon relationships changed considerably. Dealings between the overall manager of the Adult Opportunity Centers and the branch supervisors took on a totally different coloration, just as did the relations between supervisors and line staff. A colleague relationship began to emerge; group decision making became prevalent; disagreements were confronted and resolved. Supervisors worked to develop staff competency and initiative, assisted the staff in resolving problems, and offered leadership in devising tools, resources, and programs. Less and less did staff or supervisors ask for "permission" to do something, and less and less was it expected of them to do so. The office did what it conceived as necessary or helpful and then informed the hierarchy. This was a complete change from the picture in the 1962 office, and there can be little doubt that the breath of freedom wafted through the whole agency to varying degrees.

Despite the permissiveness described, the coastal area office and the state hierarchy never did enter boldly into the arena. They never developed a system which would permit them to extend staff assistance or additional support to unusual programs or techniques, even when they found them highly successful. No research was attempted to determine if and how they succeeded. No new evaluation tools were developed. No serious thought was given or resources provided to export any of the innovations. However, from sheer exposure many office managers did pick up on the signals and did make efforts to incorporate some ideas into their own operations. The workshop idea, particularly, was tried in many offices. But of all the concepts developed in the Western Addition office the workshops were the least exportable, especially into a cold, traditional setting in a daytime office with regular staff on a time schedule.

Workships, if they are not to deteriorate into lectures with an agenda on "How to Look for Work," are absolutely dependent on atmosphere, looseness, openness, and involvement. They are the most disruptive activity to the workings of a traditional office, and they require the most knowledgeable and dedicated leadership. In order to develop such leadership skills, careful selections must be made and extensive training must be provided.

The Adult Opportunity Center experience remained essentially an aberration, outside the system, affecting it in only the most insignificant way operationally. Its effect on the consciousness of staff and hierarchy may have been stronger than that, particularly with regard to the possibilities for an outreach office. After the demise of the office and the resignation of the manager, the state director expressed great indignation over the "desertion" of the manager. When the accusation was reversed and the state director was asked why the agency deserted, why the agency was unable to make the necessary decisions and take the necessary steps to sustain and possibly reproduce a program which had become a source of pride to the agency, he gave what is probably the classic answer: It simply wasn't anybody's job; nobody had been given that assignment.

A conclusion reluctantly arrived at by the more thoughtful staff members was that manpower programs were in effect acting as an umbrella to shield institutions, agencies, and the general public from knowledge about the magnitude of "people" problems that are not basically manpower problems and that can't be touched by manpower remedies. Some interviewers have estimated that as high as 50 percent of their clients were literally unable to work on any job. Not even the most sophisticated among the staff had anticipated the extent and degree of destruction of human beings in the ghettos and barrios. Only a seriously delusioned interviewer or an ego-driven counselor could maintain the myth that assigning a heroin addict to an MDTA slot or placing a pimp in a $2.50 an hour job was sufficient inducement to drop the addiction or the "hustle." The inability of the severe alcoholic or the gambling addict to deal with the work or training situation left the interviewer helpless. Job after job was obtained for a man and was lost. Hustle after hustle was perpetrated on staff and office.

No amount of compassion could disguise the magnitude of the problem.

The interviewer felt certain that all the resources he could muster, all the heartfelt effort he could pour in, all the knowledge and talent he had were grossly inadequate. And despite his sometimes heroic efforts, he became equally certain that he could not successfully manipulate existing institutions to extend themselves in order to incorporate his client. He could not avoid the feeling that much of what he did was futile and wasteful. Repeatedly, staff members expressed the hope that manpower policy makers would come to grips with these realities and develop an explicit policy and alternative programs, rather than try to make all problems fit into a manpower program. But it was left to the interviewer to grapple with. Sitting at the lowest point on the ladder, he was forced to make his own policy and seek his own solutions for these severe victims of oppression while policy makers engaged in compassionate rhetoric.

Although each staff member assumed the role of ombudsman for his clients, it became very clear that the staff's collective efforts resulted in very little success in obtaining "supportive services" from existing agencies. Referring a person to another agency is easy. Actually getting the person into the program or getting a service is quite another thing. Despite extensive efforts, very few clients actually got into the vocational rehabilitation program, very few were accepted for treatment at the Center for Special Problems, very few were accepted as appropriate cases at the Legal Services for the Poor offices . . . and welfare eligibility rules were rigid. The county hospital was still the only source of medical help; to obtain a new set of teeth for a client required hours of interviewer scrounging. Despite a close working relationship with the police department's community relations unit, only a tiny number of applicants with arrest records were actually helped with that problem.

It was clear that the search for sufficient supportive services in the community was a relatively unproductive one for the office, compared to its effectiveness when developing its own responsive programs and providing those services and that fund of labor market information that the office itself organized.

There was no doubt that the office was a remarkable catalyst — a change mechanism for those individuals who were intimately involved with it, whether served or serving, on either side of the encounter. And it left some kind of mark on bureaucratic perceptions.

What remained very much in doubt is whether manpower problems are at all amenable to an individualized service approach. Those advocates of incentive pay to staff members who argue that a man will work hard and effectively only if he is paid on a commission basis for every disadvantaged person placed on the job would have been hard put to defend their philosophy if they watched the staff work in that Victorian house. Their assertions belittle the backbreaking, heartbreaking efforts of those individuals to whom a twelve-hour day was a frequent event — without overtime pay. No one could have worked harder or with more ingenuity and cunning than did that staff. The most that could have been done with the resources was done, and there *were* successes. But it became a certainty, however difficult to face, that none of the manpower programs, none of the efforts of the Adult Opportunity Center could significantly affect the external realities. The efforts were as seedlings before a hurricane. The center, despite its gargantuan effort, remained essentially a buffer operation, a ghetto rage cooler.

The Adult Opportunity Center could do many remarkable things, but in the final recokoning it could not change the world for the disadvantaged, and it could not change the disadvantaged for the world.

EARLY 1970s:
The Local Office Revisited

Between 1966 and 1970, manpower training programs proliferated considerably. The power struggle over who would deliver the programs was clearly resolved in favor of the Department of Labor, and discrete programs, even those that had been formerly administered by other subcontractors, were increasingly reassigned to the employment service system. New acronyms emerged — CEP, a concentrated employment program focused on target areas of most intense poverty, the National Alliance of Business' Job Opportunities in the Business Sector program (NAB-JOBS), New Careers, institutional and on-the-job training programs under MDTA, Job Corps, the manpower component of the Model Cities program. All of these programs became wholly or partially the responsibility of the employment service and as such were resources for the staff in dealing with the unemployed. In 1968 Congress passed an amendment to the Social Security Act known as the Work Incentive program (WIN). It mandated the employment service to provide intensive "employability development" services for eligible welfare clients under the Aid to Families with Dependent Children program. Concepts such as "employability plans" and the team approach, which emanated from the Work Incentive program, permeated the agency.

The stance of the national agency was increasingly one of service in all functions for all people and all segments of the economy. The placement function was declared to be the key objective. But simultaneously manpower development rather than labor exchange was declared to be the primary concern. Employment offices were to become comprehensive manpower centers. And local offices in many areas of the country went through the paces of changing their names to various types of manpower centers, presumably redesigning staff jobs and functions, and applying the new terminology. "Completion" became "assessment," and "counseling" became "employability development."

Changes in California and San Francisco

In California, the Human Resources Development Act (AB 1463) was supported by both Democrats and Republicans, each for their own reasons. It was passed by the legislature and signed into law by Governor Ronald Reagan in August 1968, for activation in October 1969. When the law was passed in 1968 the unemployment rate in California was 4.5 percent. By the time the second phase of the changeover was completed in January 1971, the unemployment rate in California was 7.0 percent. In effect, the law was never fully implemented, and many of its injunctions and provisions fell into disuse or proved to be illusory or inoperable. One of those who participated in designing the act declared plaintively a few years later: "We were double crossed by the economy."

In a sense, the passage of the Human Resources Development Act and the subsequent events contain elements of classic tragedy and embody the struggles, hopes, victories, and misconceptions of the decade. The highest motives intermingle with the basest, the great moment of victory already telegraphing the inexorable defeat. For those who had struggled long and hard to turn the employment service into a vehicle that was of some value to the poor and black, it should have been a moment of victory when the largest state in the union established, as public policy, that the agency direct its major resources toward the most severely disadvantaged population. And yet, both within and without the agency, dedicated individuals who had intimate knowledge of the 1960s deplored the act and anticipated its unworkability. For one thing, the legislature mandated what should be done with moneys it didn't control — resources produced by a directly conflicting federal mandate. But even more important, the act itself was filled with such extensive administrative intervention, was so lacking in knowledge about the agency's experiences during the previous decade, was so naive in concept, and was so shallow in understanding of the manpower arena as to appear deliberately programmed for failure and counterproductivity. Apparently, little had been learned from experience, and even less had been applied. "Pet" ideas and untested schemes took the place of serious thought or knowledge. What is even more incomprehensible, a vehicle already existed which had been established by the legislature for state intervention into the employment service system with specific orientation toward the disadvantaged — the State Service Center program. Whatever flaws there were, it was a functioning entity, but its existence was largely ignored by the legislature when it passed AB 1463.

Strange alliances were made, and conflicting ideologies appeared to join hands. Liberal rhetoric and conservative business ethics became confused and intertwined. "Good guys" became "bad guys" overnight, and those previously regarded as racists joined forces with black militants. Without a doubt, that factor which unified so many disparate elements was the assault on the employment service, either for not doing enough or for doing too much. It was an attempt, through legislation, to change a state agency. And yet, the passage of the act and the subsequent reorganization of the agency did bring about some new ideas. It did establish a solid minority identification. And it did elicit considerable personal vigor. In fact, the single most important contribution of the new legislation and the "new" approach was to bring minority group members into leadership positions through the employment service itself.

One of the peculiarities of the act was that it departed from the policy-making role and attempted to mandate what were essentially administrative functions. The keystone to a unified manpower service delivery system, as described in the act, was a new civil service category called the "job agent," to whom severely disadvantaged persons would be referred. It was the job agent who was defined as the symbol of commitment to help the poor people escape poverty. The act not only established the position of job agent, it also defined the duties and tools of his job. These included the development of a training and employability plan, the procurement of training and related services, review and evaluation of individual progress, postemployment followup, and assistance in overcoming obstacles.

What was perhaps most serious in terms of operational consequences was that the legislation spelled out a very specific method for dealing with these disadvantaged individuals. The job agent would have "case responsibility," a concept lifted bodily from other social agencies where the model had been operating with dubious success and grafted onto the manpower operation — by legal mandate. While the casework concept had been tried in the Service Center program, there it had been introduced by counselors from the various other agencies and disciplines on a voluntary basis, not by mandate from above. Even so, the clear lack of success of that effort was not a deterrent to framers of the Human Resources Development Act. In their minds, the presence of the job agent would make the case method work.

One can try to imagine the rationale used by the designers of the Human Resources Development Act. Perhaps they transplanted the casework orientation in order to institutionalize accountability. The agency and its staff, they might have reasoned, would be made finally accountable for its activities. Casework requires extensive writeups — a careful detailing of the problems and the actions taken for each person dealt with. Perhaps the designers of the act sought to prescribe a tool which would ensure a broader scope of responsibility and wider goals for the agency, other than simply job matching. Perhaps they wanted to legalize advocacy, commitment, kindness, and service on the part of the staff. The framers may have been unaware that good people had always existed in the agency and had found ways to function in that fashion, even when the employment service was totally employer oriented and no matter how limited the time or how disapproving the agency might have been. There is hardly an interviewer who hasn't managed, sometimes sneakily, to perform acts of personal service or referral to another agency for a needful applicant. But in 1962 such activity was semilegal and undercover. The Human Resources Development Act, by prescribing the social worker technique, attempted to sanction this type of activity in California. Official sanction, however, had come well before the passage of the act. That step had already been taken; that wheel had been invented. It was already known that all the sanction in the world would not create outlets, resources, or potency.

Questions around the casework notion go to the very heart of the manpower emphasis of the 1960s and the model legislated by the Human Resources Development Act. Although this subject has been dealt with earlier, the persistent recurrence historically provokes further discussion. The matter of appropriateness again arises. To many who had been in the field, it was already clear that the massive emphasis on the social services orientation enunciated by the California Legislature was particularly unfitting and ineffectual in the manpower arena. Neither in the consciousness of the person coming to the agency for assistance nor in the actual solution to that person's problem is the service element a significant factor. It is, at best, a minor one, hovering on the periphery of the central issues. The fact is that many individuals work steadily even though they have endless personal problems, medical difficulties, psychological maladjustments, problems with addiction, arrest records, low literacy, and family problems. Many of these things occur to even the most successful in our society. And although such problems are certainly rife among the disadvantaged unemployed, it is possible that they would assume secondary significance if the economy offered good jobs, training resources, extensive child-care facilities, or other income-producing alternatives with some relationship to the actual need.

The situation is analogous to social worker attitudes surrounding the unwed mother. For many years her condition was regarded by Freudian-dominated social work professionals as an expression of a disturbed and sick psyche, qualitatively different from the psyche of the woman who engaged in extramarital sexual activity and didn't get pregnant or the married woman with an unwanted pregnancy. If one looked at the unwed mother with that orientation, one unquestionably found evidence that she suffered from disturbed psychological processes. But the degree to which these psychological factors were important became very suspect, indeed, as the pill, greater availability of abortions, and changed social attitudes toward the unwed mother became more widespread. When reality solutions and a change in social climate appeared, the continuation of the institutions and treatment processes which were based on the "sick" definition of the unwed mother became clearly passe. This leaves us to wonder about the original diagnosis. Was the "sickness" of the mother ever the most significant explanation for the unwanted pregnancy? Is the "sickness" of ghetto residents the most significant explanation for the disadvantaged state? It is difficult to isolate the problems of the disadvantaged from the real absence of opportunities in the total social environment. Which is the cause and which is the effect? *That* is unclear.

Other questions evolve from the casework concept and its application to the manpower field. Most of these questions were already being asked because of the history with Adult Opportunity Centers, Youth Opportunity Centers, manpower training programs, and the State Service Center program. All of these had strong elements of personalized social services.

Is the casework method the best way to achieve advocacy and deliver personal services? Are there better, less costly, and less destructive ways to perform realistic services for a person? It is not at all clear that there are no alternatives or that the caseload method ensures accountability and action. What it certainly does is reinforce the least desirable qualities in staff members and impose an enormous amount of unproductive paper work. It is of dubious value to the job seeker, especially when the staff has no resources, no money, no nothing. The temptation to overpromise is great, and the temptation to be overpromised is even greater. (It is almost always assumed by the "case" that all the paper work means something good must happen in the end.) And of course, here again the same situation obtains as has been discussed earlier: the utter absence of leverage by manpower interviewers, even job agents, to obtain services from other agencies. This absence of power underlines the questionable value of the approach.

Whether the job agent program would have worked, given resources to provide needed services, will never be known. Funds for the job agent to "buy" services for his client were authorized but never appropriated. Thus, the job agent had precisely the same resources available for the disadvantaged as the interviewer had in the Adult Opportunity Center offices — and much less experience.

The most interesting example of ideological confusion that permeated the Human Resources Development Act was that section of the law which provided that job agents were to be compensated on the basis of their achievement in obtaining successful completion of training and employment goals of eligible persons. In plain words, job agents were to be paid on a commission basis as soon as job performance standards were developed. Continuous employment of the individual for eighteen months was defined as the criterion by which a job agent's success with a client would be judged. The private employment agency model was to become the model for dealing with the poor in a state agency.

This was a direct insult to employment service staff members who had been in the ghetto offices; it was a slap in the face. Even more, it violated everything they had learned. It was as if the state legislature was saying that the explanation for the presumed failure to place and keep black or disadvantaged individuals in the jobs was the indifference and callousness of the regular staff, and the only way that an interviewer could be motivated to place a man on a job and *make* him stay there for over eighteen months was to give the interviewer a new title and a money incentive — commissions. The realities of the secondary labor market and its behavior didn't count. Apparently, the thinking was that private employment agencies successfully made placements because they used the commission system; the same system should be used with the job agents, paying a commission on the basis of a graduated scale of "difficulty to place." Some sort of job performance standards was to be developed which allowed so much "credit" for each placement, so much more if a man had one felony conviction, more if he had two felony convictions, and so on.

(This incentive pay system was never made operational and has apparently been abandoned. The employability rating study which would have established the basis for paying the commission was never completed. Interestingly, the job agents themselves were among those most vigorously opposed to the installation of incentive pay. For a time, an attempt was made to invite voluntary participation in the incentive pay program, but the response was so feeble that the attempt was dropped. The California Assembly's Office of Research did a study of the job agent program in 1972 in which it blamed the demise of the program on such factors as the absence of casework funds, the absence of incentive pay, the general direction of the agency away from concern for the disadvantaged, and the inability of the bureaucracy to incorporate the concept of individualized service. The report did not question the validity of the job agent concept, and it recommended that the program instituted by the Human Resources Development Act be continued.)

In such a fashion was it possible to weld a social and humanistic goal for black inclusion with the popular wisdom of private enterprise that only the financial motivation is an operating factor in human endeavor. In the name of "progressive" social policy, it was possible to absolve the economic and social power of the country for its failure to incorporate the black population into economic life and lay the blame, instead, at the door of the lowest and most vulnerable echelon of the establishment structure — the helpless, impotent, and voiceless interviewer in a local office of the employment service. The agency whose role had been that of a buffer was given the job agent as a buffer for the buffer. It was his responsibility to rid the state of the impoverished and excluded. And it became possible for the agency to point to the job agents for their preordained failure.

Administratively, the act dissolved the Department of Employment and substituted the Department of Human Resources Development. The new department incorporated what had previously been four entities: the Department of Employment, the State Department of Economic Opportunity, the State Service Center program, and the Commission on Aging.

The goals of the new agency were stated:

> Enable employable and potentially employable persons in California, who are economically disadvantaged, to reach and maintain a level of economic sufficiency, and assist other employable persons in maintaining economic stability through job training, placement and related services, unemployment insurance and disability insurance.

Clearly, the goals were lofty and commendable, but they had little to do with reality and were, therefore, unattainable.

Another important feature of the Human Resources Development Act provided that offices were to be established in the economically disadvantaged areas designated by the director according to a formula provided by the act. The offices were to be known as Human Resources Development Centers. Eligibility criteria were established for disadvantaged persons based on higher income levels than those established by the federal government.

The administration also reorganized and restructured the former Department of Employment. It eliminated the area office concept and the division of the state into four parts. Instead, the state was divided into two regions — the northern and southern regions.

It would be an exercise in futility to describe the new administration in detail and the reorganization of the agency following the implementation of the Human Resources Development Act. Since that time there have been at least two more regimes and two more reorganizations. From early 1970 to the latter part of 1972, the employment service staff underwent organizational restructuring and the installation of a new group of top administrations three different times.

The important thing for our purposes is to understand the atmosphere in which the local office functioned in 1970. The Human Resources Development Act and its implementation split the agency line offices and the hierarchy into two distinct and hostile camps. This was not only true in atmosphere, it was true, in some respects, structurally. The discrete manpower programs such as the Work Incentive program and the Concentrated Employment program often operated with their own internal administrative structures, which further added to the sense that the agency resembled an umbrella under which a number of separated entities functioned, often conflicting and competing.

One agency, created by a combination of the California act and federally funded manpower programs, was entirely focused on serving the disadvantaged and was administered and manned primarily by staff members from minority races. The other, the traditional employment service agency, funded and mandated by Wagner-Peyser Title III funds, was by that time staffed almost completely with white workers and was greatly reduced in numbers. It served the rest of the population in the central cities and in the smaller communities, and it maintained some focus on serving the employers. Simultaneously, unemployment was rising dramatically, especially among white blue-collar workers and professionals.

An entirely new roster of administrators was appointed from outside the agency. These individuals had no knowledge or experience in the manpower field. This was accomplished through a series of executive appointments exempted from the civil service system. Because the "enemy" had been defined by the new policy makers as the regular employment service and the "bad guys" were those identified with the previous administrative structure from the director on down, the new administration saw it as a major goal to rid the agency of all previous influences and proceed with reinvention, rediscovery, and redesign. Old staff members were seen as sources of doubtful information and advice; they were to be distrusted and sometimes humiliated. Many resigned. It was, indeed, paradoxical that the very agency and individuals who had scribed the widest arc in the entire Department of Labor network of state agencies, who had made the most extensive push into converting their operation toward an orientation to the disadvantaged, came to be the primary target of black legislators, black civil service administrators in state government, old and new liberal groups, and a Republican, business-dominated state government administration.

Thirteen Human Resources Development Centers were established in northern California. In San Francisco the picture of agency installations in 1970 was as follows: The three remaining Adult Opportunity Center offices had been enlarged, converted, or moved to bigger quarters and redesignated as Human Resources Development Centers. The State Service Center in the Western Addition remain. One Youth Opportunity Center office remained. A separate Work Incentive (WIN) office existed. A separate Concentrated Employment (CEP) office existed, which was later split into six reporting units. And the two old downtown offices remained, the industrial and service office and the commercial and professional office. In all, there were ten installations in San Francisco. Of the 383 individuals who worked in the local offices, 300 worked in the Human Resources Development Centers, the WIN and CEP offices, the State Service Center, and the Youth Opportunity Center. Only 83 employees remained in the two regular downtown employment service offices, approximately the same number as in 1962.

In keeping with the mandate of the Human Resources Development Act, all manpower training programs were allocated to the nontraditional offices. Staffing patterns in the two "agencies" are worth exploring because they telegraph the inevitable consequences of a two-agency concept. Most of the experienced journeymen of the agency, the classification known as employment security officer I, remained with the employment service offices, either by their own choice or because they were regarded as unacceptable in attitude, color, and training for the other offices.

The bulk of the staff in the Human Resource Development centers and the State Service Centers were either newly trained employment security officers or paraprofessionals. In San Francisco eight job agents were hired, many from outside the agency. Almost all were members of minority groups and were located in the four Human Resources Development Center offices. All of the newly appointed center managers were minority group members. The two regular employment service office managers were white.

Every decision appeared to be designed to increase the chasm between the old staff members and the new, to ensure the resistance and anger of the traditional staff, rather than to gain its support. For example, the new director of the agency fought for and won the right to have all of the Human Resources Development Center managers designated in civil service terms as career executive appointments. The results were that newly appointed managers received considerably more money than the old-time managers, and what is even more devastating, were in a much higher administrative position in the bureaucratic hierarchy. Thus, the supervisory and technical assistance structure of the traditional agency found itself at the same level as — or even lower than — the individuals they were supposed to supervise or assist. Salaries of newly appointed job agents were set at a level equivalent to that of the second level supervisory staff, the employment security officer II, who supervised entire units in the 1962 office. This was considerably higher than that of a journeyman who had been with the agency for ten years. Again, the job agents were beyond the supervision of the usual structure. And when their proposed incentive pay plan did not materialize, when the authorized casework funds were not appropriated, the job agent became indistinguishable from any other interviewer, except that he received a great deal more money for the same work. This was hardly designed to make him a figure to win the love of the rest of the staff.

(By early 1973 *all* the local offices in San Francisco were named Human Resources Development Centers, and some effort had been made to equalize the pay of managers. Still, some salary discrepancies continued. The split administrative structure had been reconciled. Unfortunately, at that time there remained only a few minority representatives at the top administrative level, either in the central office in Sacramento or at the regional level.)

The agency was split on every conceivable basis — along racial lines, along the lines of old and new loyalties, along the lines of compensation, along the lines of allocated resources. The arrangement could only generate smoldering resentments. One "agency" perceived the other as overstaffed, overrated, overpaid — a "do-nothing" operation. The other "agency" regarded the mainline operation as stiltified, incipiently racist, incompetent, and unreliable.

Initially, the regional office reflected and generated this spirit. The new regional director, a black man from the education field, set about to develop the new Human Resources Development Centers and turned the old-line agency operation over to the former coastal division manager, who had become the regional director's subordinate. The director himself assumed responsibility for the staffing and supervision of the newly defined Human Resources Development Centers and other poverty area installations. The old coastal area staff was in communication with the new regional administrators only on the most tenuous of terms.

One of the operating principles that came into being was "management by objectives," which meant the decentralization of powers from Sacramento to the regional offices and downward to the local offices. Although this was primarily intended to free the newly appointed Human Resources Development Center managers from the traditional bureaucratic constraints, the effects went further. The instructions were clear to all office managers: "Let the managers manage." Regional staff was seen as a technical service *for* the managers, but the managers were encouraged to reexamine their activities and to make significant decisions regarding the emphasis and workings of their own offices. Whatever other confusion and misdirection was rampant, the effect of this concept was pervasive in an agency that, despite its already loosened bureaucratic controls, was still a traditional bureaucracy. Generally, the effect was positive because a period of reexamination and reappraisal was possible. It was in that atmosphere that the Hayward experiment, with its revolutionary concepts of manpower services, became a possibility. (See Chapter 5 for a complete description of the Hayward operation.) It was because of that atmosphere and the particular understanding of the new regional director that all northern California offices developed the Job Information Centers with their open orders and cafeteria-style service.

However, decentralization of decision-making power coupled with the emphasis on the managers' right to manage did produce some distressing results. For example, since the managers were endowed with such power, the newly staffed Human Resources Development Centers took on the quality of unassailable fortresses in the eyes of the rest of the agency. The centers were subject to minimal supervision, contained minimal skills, experience, and knowledge, and seemed to have little access to or desire for whatever competency resided in the old-line agency.

The Hayward experiment was viewed by Human Resources Development Center managers as something that belonged to the old-line agency, rather than as a possible delivery system which could be of value to the centers. On one occasion, the director of the regional office and the manager of the Mission Human Resources Development Center (a center located in the predominantly Spanish-speaking community) agreed to begin the process of installing the Hayward experiment in that center. Shortly after the transition process began, the center manager was transferred and a new manager was installed. He used his prerogatives to scrap the experiment.

To a degree, this was understandable and even predictable. The Hayward experiment set out to change the goals and mission of the agency in a particular direction, and the delivery system model reflected that direction. The main ideas for the experiment sprang from those individuals who had already experienced the frustrations and failures that attended the path of "supportive services," casework, and "employability development." The concepts of Hayward sprang from years of experience with the traps in the placement count and employer emphasis, and with the inherently discriminatory patterns of a job-matching model.

However, the Hayward experiment was in direct variance with the mandate of the Human Resources Development Act, which clearly defined the route to change and redesign as being through the casework method. The Human Resources Development Center managers were new, and they followed the law and the managers' handbook, a book which described a model for a Human Resources Development Center and which rested almost entirely on an individualized service involving various levels of case responsibility. The manager of one Human Resources Development Center decided to put everyone on a case load basis. After a short while a job seeker had to wait three weeks to see anyone because the case loads were full.

The managers' handbook provided an interesting definition of eligible clients: "A person who suffers economic deprivation and is employable or capable of being made employable through services provided or arranged by the Human Resources Development Center." Such a definition so glibly stated begs the questions about who is or is not "employable," what method the centers would use to make someone "employable," or what power or resources the center had to· provide services from outside the center to make someone "employable." These questions had remained unresolved in the experiences of those who had already been confronting the problem for three years.

The managers' handbook also presented a concept called an "economic sufficiency plan." This provided a blueprint for individualized services, including the steps necessary to "move a person from joblessness or underemployment to permanent adequate employment which will provide him a standard of living substantially above the poverty line." This would seem to be quite a task in view of the fact that large numbers of employed persons never get "substantially above the poverty line." Each disadvantaged person coming into a center was to have such a plan developed with and for him by a case responsible person. That was to be the blueprint by which the man was to be moved into "economic sufficiency." It was also the plan to which the interviewer or job agent would be held accountable.

The model for a Human Resources Development Center was rooted in a perfectly logical assembly line operation, with job seekers "assessed" at the beginning of the path, categorized, set on various tracks, and helped along to their "economic sufficiency" goals by the case responsible person. And they were supposed to come out at the other end, all shiny red or blue, depending on what track they had been on, or who turned what screw, or what part had been oiled. This was supposed to happen . . . in a period of 7 percent unemployment. It was Never-Never Land, an elaborate concept with everyone playing the game, pretending it was real, pretending that he could really exert such influence and power. Again, all the form was there but not a breath of content. In the center of this assembly line sat the most important fixer-upper — the job agent. All the deprivation, all the madness wrought by three hundred years of oppression, all the indifference of a huge and powerful industrial society . . . were going to be made right by one person, the job agent.

Was ever an idea more cynically considered or more naively propounded or more clearly doomed to defeat?

The Hayward direction and the direction set out by the Human Resources Development Act for the centers were inimical, and the new center managers saw them as such. Not so, however, in the regional office. The new regional director perceived the inadequacies of both the model created by the state legislature and the traditional job-matching model; he enthusiastically and vigorously undertook the experiment in Hayward. It was a wise decision, because more than any single activity the Hayward experiment had a unifying effect on the agency in San Francisco. Old and new staffs in the region learned to work together, and the regional director came to value the traditional knowledge and skills. Old-line staff members were deeply gratified by the courage exhibited by the regional director, and it is entirely to his credit that the chasm of distrust began to close, at least at that level. His emphasis was increasingly on the development of mechanisms for reintegrating the agency — conceptually, functionally, and racially. Early in his tenure he came to the belief that old employment service skills were of some value, even in the ghetto office. He began to feel that people in the ghetto were more in need of someone who talked authoritatively and knowledgeably to employers than they were in need of "soul" talk and "rapport."

However, nothing could serve to unify the purposes and goals of the agency when faced with conflicting federal and state mandates and a changing economy. As unemployment rose, especially among the professional and technical occupations, the pressures came from the Department of Labor regional office and from various groups in the state. The emphasis on placement count was renewed. (There is a peculiar and profound illogic that seemes to pervade the manpower field, whatever the focus. As jobs become scarcer and scarcer, the demand is made on the agency to make more and more placements. Once again, it is that incredible assumption of power, of capacity to change a direction of the economy. It is difficult to imagine what miracle was expected of the agency that could assist the "job ready" when the unemployment rate was 7 percent.)

One other development in 1970 illustrates the peculiar mixture of the times and points up the inherent dichotomies. It also reflects interestingly on the job agent concept. A demonstration project was funded by the Office of Economic Opportunity whereby the Division of Human Resources Development would compete with private employment agencies to determine comparative capability for placing welfare clients on jobs. The project was intensely opposed by some community action agencies and by the labor movement. The purpose of the project was to assess the potential of profit-making private employment agencies to place the disadvantaged, and then to make comparisons between the private agencies and public programs based on a cost-benefit analysis. The saving of welfare dollars was taken as the direct measure of public benefits. It was the aim of the project to determine whether the profit incentive concepts of private employment services were an effective resource for the disadvantaged population. The project was seen as similar in some respects to the voucher system in education. If the experiment succeeded in establishing that the cost of the private employment agency was comparable to the exclusive use of the public placement services, the director would be able to request transfer of available funds to support the program. In short, the public employment service and the private employment agencies were to engage in a contest to determine which could be most effective in placing welfare clients. Not only was it a contest, but there was a substantial "purse" for the winner.

The project was designed to operate in four major counties: San Francisco, San Diego, Orange, and Los Angeles. The design called for social welfare departments to refer "job ready" clients to the Human Resources Development installations. The Human Resources Development staffs were to select approximately twelve hundred clients on a random basis. All clients were to be categorized on the basis of an employability rating system. The classification would establish the probability of placement on a scale graduated low, medium, and high. Selected clients from all three categories would be sent to the private employment agencies, which would be required to place the individuals within 45 days. If unsuccessful, the agencies would "return" the job seekers to the Human Resources Development Center. If successful, the private agencies would be compensated on a pay schedule based on placements that lasted for thirty days and more, with a double fee for placements of individuals rated lowest on the probability scale. Fees were set at a generous level.

The employment service staff reacted negatively to this contest. They felt strongly that the contest was inherently unequal, since the public agency was committed to "people" and the private agencies were committed to fees. Perhaps there was some fear that the odds were against the employment service. Counselors pointed out that they were oriented to the welfare of the individual beyond placement on any particular job and that private agencies would likely "sell" a job to an individual which was actually unsuited to him or well beneath his potential in order to collect a fee. Others seriously doubted the equity of the project design, pointing to the fact that the private employment agencies' costs would be determined only in relation to the 45 days for which they had responsibility to the client, while the Human Resources Development offices' costs extended over the entire period that the client was a part of the work load. Still other employees of the agency were concerned about the possibility of employer collusion during the contest, especially in cases where the employer paid the agency fees.

The most serious concerns arose from the knowledge staff workers had gained from experience which indicated that private agencies were discriminatory and exploitive. This was a conclusion arrived at after listening to hundreds of applicants describe their own experiences with private agencies, but there was also considerable objective evidence for this conclusion. A job placement survey was conducted by the Anti-Defamation League in the Los Angeles area in 1967. A mock job order for a white, Protestant stenographer was placed in 86 private agencies and six public employment service installations. Of the 86 private agencies, fourteen were members of the California Employment Agencies Association, which had made several efforts to secure voluntary compliance by its member agencies to a code forbidding such discriminatory practices. Seventy-five of the private agencies (87 percent) accepted the order. All six public employment service installations refused the order on the ground that discriminatory specifications were against the law. (The state Fair Employment Practices Act passed in 1959 made the acceptance of such an order illegal for any employment agency.)

Such practices were not unusual in private employment agencies. And better than any other segment of society, the employment service staff understood why such practices were so widespread, so persistent, and so insidious. It was for reasons which were much more intrinsic than simple race discrimination. Private job placement agencies depended totally upon receiving and satisfying job orders from employers. The individual working for a private agency had to remain in the good graces of the employers to protect his own personal income; he was inherently unable to act as an agent of social change or to do anything but accept and follow well behind the hiring standards and practices of the employer community. Surely, no private employment interviewer with a "list" of exclusive employers would risk jeopardizing future income by going out of his way to find a precarious placement for a disadvantaged person.

Despite these factors — or because of them — when the contest was over and the report was finally released (it was suppressed for some time), the Human Resources Development Centers won hands down. The initial draft of an evaluation study showed that the Division of Human Resources Development gave the superior performance in most of the factors examined. The final report, which was watered down somewhat from the original version, showed that the Department of Human Resources Development placed 22.26 percent of the welfare clients, while the private agencies placed 7.3 percent of their test population. The average cost for the Human Resources Development Centers was $190.83 per placement. The average cost per placement for the private agencies was $250.76. (Even in the face of such statistics, the report stated that the results were "inconclusive.")

It was amid this turmoil, this confusion, and this conflict that the local employment service offices operated in San Francisco in 1970. It is well worth revisiting the local office to see what changes occurred between 1962 and 1970.

The Local Office Revisited: Industrial and Services Office, 1970

There was still a counter in the 1970 industrial and services office, and there was still a receptionist. And the building was a formidable bureaucractic structure. But there was a major difference from the 1962 office. On the public side of the counter was something of value, something the public most wanted — access to the jobs themselves.

A Job Information Center was required in all northern California local offices by 1970. In the industrial and services office it occupied the lobby area. It displayed the open job orders, although the employers' names and addresses were obscured. The job orders were wrapped in cellophane and hung on the walls under occupational headings. The area was open to the public and it was not necessary to be registered for work in order to use the Job Information Center. Anyone could walk in and look at the jobs listed.

A sign in the lobby directed visitors to complete a form provided in order to obtain additional information about any job listed. No staff person was stationed on the public side of the counter. In addition to the job listings, the area had some displays and some pamphlets and posters providing occupational and industrial information. Every job order obtained by the office was displayed, except for domestic day work. The Job Information Center was a self-screening operation in which the office supplied the referral information at the request of the applicant.

The receptionist working behind the counter seldom had any lines in front of him. The Job Information Center allowed job seekers to examine the jobs without waiting in line; many came and left without addressing any member of the staff. Also, the existence of the four outreach Human Resources Development Centers, the Youth Opportunity Center, and the casual labor offce had significantly reduced the applicant flow. Over and above all of this, statistics indicated there were fewer people using the employment service throughout the state than there were a decade earlier.

The job seeker was allowed to fill out a work application if he wished, but he was cautioned that his best chance of getting work was by checking the job boards regularly, and there was no promise that he would be contacted. However, application cards were solicited from veterans, from the handicapped, and from applicants eligible for programs designed for the disadvantaged. The application card was coded to reflect these factors. The receptionist made an educated guess about whether the applicant was or was not eligible for designation as a disadvantaged person. As was the case a decade earlier, the application card was to be completed by the applicant, and a completion interviewer provided the clarification and coding. In addition to the options that the completion interviewer had in 1962 — including referral to a placement interviewer or to any of the services for special applicant groups — the 1970 completion interviewer could also refer an eligible applicant to one of two human resources development specialists. Applicants from minority groups who were considered job ready were referred to the minority employment representative.

The human resources development specialists to whom the disadvantaged were referred each carried a case load of about two hundred clients. The activities of the specialists were described as providing "in-depth interviewing" and "supportive services." The term "supportive services" translated into attempts by the human resources development specialists to arrange needed services through existing public institutions and agencies such as the Salvation Army social services, vocational rehabilitation, and so on. This was the same kind of referral service that many interviewers provided in 1962, although at that time it was mildly illegitimate.

Most specialists admitted that even though the activity was sanctioned in 1970, the resources were meager.

Job development in the traditional meaning met with more success, and a good deal more of it went on in the industrial and services office than was usually evident in outreach centers. The specialists in the downtown office were usually experienced interviewers who had considerable familiarity with the market.

Few resources were available to the office to support the "people" focus of the agency. As mentioned earlier, an administrative decision had been made in accordance with the Human Resources Development Act to allocate *all* manpower training slots to the centers located in poverty communities. It should be made clear, however, that despite the existence of offices in poverty areas, the clientele of this particular downtown office also encompassed large numbers of minority applicants in low-skill occupations.

The activities of the veterans representative had undergone some change since 1962 because of the flow of returning veterans from Vietnam and the presence of the Job Information Center. The veterans representative had a large applicant file which he checked against new orders before the orders were placed on the public board. He was often caught between the disapproval of the veterans representative, who considered the Job Information Centers a threat to the veterans preference mandate, and the criticism of the local office administrators, who were eager to keep faith with the public regarding the promise to put *all* jobs on the board.

The minority employment representative, a position established in 1964 in all California local offices, was charged with the responsibility for matching skilled jobs with minority applicants. The enforcement of state and federal regulations against discrimination and the change in public consciousness had apparently reduced the need for this type of effort on the part of the minority employment representative; if anything, the demand for skilled minority workers was far greater than the supply. As a result, the minority employment representative was involved in a good deal of community contact work, and he represented the office at community antidiscrimination activities.

The concept of counseling had undergone dramatic change in the employment service during the decade. To what degree these new concepts were operating successfully in a regular local office depended largely on the quality and training of the individual counselor, the atmosphere in the office, and the population it served. Since the counselor was required to have a master's degree in counseling or thirty units in counselor-related subjects, the department training revolved less around counseling and more on developing labor market understanding and defining the counselor role in the employment service setting. Stemming from the shift of policy toward services for the disadvantaged, the agency emphasis was less on occupational selection and more on awareness of symptomatology, on motivational work, and on imparting this awareness to the rest of the staff. In an office such as the industrial office, the staff was more apt to refer to the counselor those applicants who were poor or black or who manifested behavior problems — the over-frequent visitor, the man arriving drunk. The decision about who saw a counselor was often a pragmatic one. The counselor was the last resort when the regular interviewers didn't know what to do with an individual.

With this kind of "feeder" system operating, it was inevitable that the bulk of counseling cases involved addiction of various kinds — alcoholics, drug addicts, and what one counselor referred to as "welfare addicts." There were emotionally and mentally disturbed individuals of all kinds — recent dischargees from mental institutions and prisons, mental retardees, and others. Many counselors were perfectly aware that their own training and the resources which they could tap were inadequate to deal with these problems. They saw themselves in the advocacy role for obtaining mental health services, squeezing a counselee into a methadone clinic, or arranging for whatever assistance the community might have to offer.

The complaint of administrators was that all too often counselors engaged in psychotherapy with their clients. This appeared to the administrators to be less than "productive" activity. At the same time, the counseling philosophy of the agency was focused on developing the client's capacity to help himself. The agency had moved strongly in the direction of group work for counselors, and some administrators expressed serious doubt about whether counselors should be retained who refused to develop group activity or who considered themselves unsuited to this type of counseling. The great emphasis on group work was also generated by the development of Work Incentive (WIN) teams in which the counselor was required to work in a staff group situation which called upon similar group interaction aptitudes. This whole concept was indeed a distance removed from the singular, one-to-one emphasis of the early 1960s when the counselor's work was done in private. Group work was a different kind of exposure for the counselor, and some resistance to it was understandable.

In the industrial and services office there was very little traditional counseling, and almost all activities of counselors consisted of supportive work. No group work was being conducted, although the office had had some previous group experience with a few counselors who had passed through the office and developed interactive groups among applicants who reflected their own particular bent. At times, workshops had been conducted for the purpose of helping applicants develop job-finding skills, but these workshops were originated and conducted by interviewers, not counselors, and so they could not be officially counted as "group counseling."

The most important procedural changes in the office from a decade earlier were: (1) the opening of the job orders to the public, (2) the relaxation of requirements that every person file a work application, (3) the establishment of a central order taking unit, and (4) the elimination of the occupational desks, with the exceptions of four interviewers who manned the domestic placement unit, a separate casual labor office, and a part-time "desk" for the garment industry.

The entire placement unit was divided between those who dealt with applicants and those who dealt with employers. The latter group consisted of four interviewers in the central order-taking unit who were responsible for taking employer orders, putting them on the teletype to the outreach installations, controlling the referral activity from the offices, and verifying the state of orders. This group in the industrial office and its counterpart in the professional and commercial office were responsible for handling most jobs that were available to the entire network in San Francisco. That network included approximately ten installations, although this varied a bit as offices closed and opened or were combined as reporting units. (Central order taking was later totally centralized for the whole city and established as a separate administrative unit.)

The placement interviewers handled those job seekers who had selected jobs from the Job Information Center. Because the job orders received by the office were essentially for low-skill work, the office policy was to require a minimum of screening. The interviewers did some job development for those applicants who could not be referred to the job they had selected. Some file search was conducted for those orders not filled by the flow of traffic if the jobs were not substandard or required such high skills that there were no registered applicants.

The staff consisted of forty workers, approximately the same number as in the early part of the decade. (In the interim the size of the staff had grown substantially and had then been reduced again.) There were three distinct units — the Job Information Center, the placement unit, and the special service section. The last consisted of a supervising counselor, an employment counselor, two human resources development specialists, the specialist for the handicapped, the veterans employment representative, and the minorities representative. The office supervisory staff consisted of a manager, an assistant manager, two section supervisors, and five line supervisors.

It was the consensus of staff members on the front lines that the Job Information Center was an effective device. Although there were occasional complaints from employers about poor screening, in the opinion of old-time staff members such complaints were no more frequent than they had been in 1962. The severe economic turndown in 1970 makes comparison by gross placement statistics impossible, but there is empirical evidence that more job seekers obtained employment through the open job orders than would have if they hadn't had access to the orders. There is also some evidence that the orders received faster action. What astonished the staff was the frequency with which jobs were filled that were so poor that no self-respecting interviewer would have or should have conducted a file search to fill them and no interviewer would have insulted an applicant by bringing him into the office for a referral. But the job seekers searching through the meager alternatives made their own decisions. The fact was that the jobs coming through the office consisted almost entirely of unskilled labor orders, domestic work, and some service jobs. A few orders for machine operators were displayed. Because of the nature of San Francisco's economy, even in good times the industrial and services office had a limited placement potential and filled a somewhat questionable role. But during the recession of 1970, the sparseness of job orders on the board and the comparative emptiness of the lobby attested to the vulnerability of the single-mission concept and the single-model ideal for all offices. Where were the jobs to come from for an industrial office located in a nonindustrial, heavily unionized city?

In a limited way the office reflected the agency shift to an emphasis on applicant services. The staff had been severely cut back during the late 1960s in order to accommodate other installations and programs. The sluggish job market and the total absence of any manpower training resources had thrown a pall on the staff. They felt they were in the backwaters of the employment service activity. Occasionally there were spurts of initiative and innovation. For example, there had been workshops initiated to help job seekers. The participants needed information about where to look for work. The office itself developed an impressive series of mimeographed handouts which listed the names of all known employers in a number of industries in San Francisco and on the peninsula, together with the types of occupations for which they had hired. Although the workshops were no longer operating, the lists were used as needed. For example, someone looking for a welding job was given a list of employers who hired welders; an electronic assembler or technician could obtain a listing of all electronic firms. All major San Francisco restaurants were listed. And so on through a whole range of occupations and industries.

The focus of discussion at staff meetings was upon the need to help applicants, but the "how" was not resolved. The office was intrigued with the idea they found in the Hayward literature that no one who came to the office should walk out with *nothing*, but even that principle was difficult to satisfy.

Just as in the Adult Opportunity Center, the staff developed a need to have more valid and pertinent labor market information to give applicants, since there were no other resources and few jobs. Because of the Job Information Center and the changed policy regarding application cards, staff members felt they had more time to personalize the service to the job seeker. This was manifested by an increase in job development efforts and by more emphasis on offering information about the search for work.

Although the manuals were still operative in 1970, they were apparently in the process of being reorganized and rewritten in Sacramento. The staff paid little attention to manuals. Supervisors did a minimum of document evaluation. Supervisory emphasis had changed. The question supervisors were asking the staff related more to whether the applicant did indeed get the services he needed, rather than to the length of time an operation took. The placement supervisor indicated that many personnel in the office were strongly influenced by the experimental Hayward project and its written material. The feeling expressed by some of the staff was that the remaining old-line supervisors and employees would make significant, gut-level change difficult unless "sensitivity" training was used to shake up entrenched attitudes. Feelings of regret were expressed because the office had apparently lagged in innovation. The assignment of a new young manager brought some hope that the office would develop more vitality. However, discussions with various agency administrators revealed a strong question in their minds about the continued validity of the industrial services office as it was constituted.

In summary, since 1962 there had been evident changes — changes in consciousness, changes in goals, and changes in some functions. But the office had a funereal quality. There was little activity and little hope for significant change. The staff felt it was left in the backwater, outside the mainstream of the movement.

Contrasting View:
The Professional and Commercial Office, circa 1970

It should be said that the professional and commercial office presented a considerably different visage to the world from that of the industrial office. Located in a well-appointed building in the heart of the financial center, the office decor gave the impression of gentility and polite helpfulness. There was a proper regard for the sensibilities of the professional and white-collar worker. However, there was a counter, and the bureaucratic stance, although considerably muted, was nevertheless evident.

It is revealing to make a brief comparison between the industrial office viewpoint and the attitudes expressed by the manager of the downtown professional and commercial office in regard to the orientation of the agency. The financial and commercial employers of San Francisco continued to have a demand for skilled and clerical workers, even during the recession, and the particular labor market on which this office was focused was not tightly controlled by other job-matching mechanisms. This situation allowed for some employment service impact and some elbow room. In a survey conducted by the San Francisco Chamber of Commerce in 1969, approximately 30 percent of the employers responding indicated that they occasionally used the California State Employment Service when recruiting their professional, technical, clerical, and sales personnel at the entrance level. This was in marked contrast to employer response about sources of recruitment for service, skilled, semiskilled, and unskilled occupations. Only 10 to 13 percent of those employers indicated any use of the agency.

The professional and commercial office was deeply involved with the LINCS program, an experimental computerized system for matching applicant to job in the professional, technical, and highly skilled office occupations which has since been abandoned. This office also had a Job Information Center with open orders displayed in the clerical and sales occupations. The registration policy was the same as that of the industrial office, with one exception — special applications were taken for those with occupations that warranted computerization. The office had an intensive employer relations program and a heavy schedule of employer visits.

The manager saw the role of the office as one of supporting a bridge to the employer community, since no other installation had an active employer visiting program. She felt it was the responsibility of her office to provide the outreach offices with jobs. Understandably, relations with employers were a major concern of this office, and the office staff had a strong belief that these relations depended heavily on a careful screening process. As a consequence, the manager felt strongly that the Job Information Center was unproductive, wasteful, and irritating to employers, and that the policy of not taking work applications for everyone saved time for the applicant but increased the screening time of the interviewer. The staff continued to be heavily involved in screening applicants who selected their own jobs from the Job Information Center.

The manager felt that in order to complete a careful review of qualifications, a work application was necessary. Staff maintained tight control on referrals and exercised the final decision on whether or not a person would be referred. The manager stated that the old 1962 system operated primarily for the employer — getting the best person to fill his job. It was her belief that a computerized matching system operated equally well for the applicant because it worked both ways, and she looked forward to an extension of the LINCS option. Not only did the computer scan the applicant's profile against the existing jobs, but each new job was scanned against the applicant's name so long as it remained active. The office continued to direct its main focus toward the placement function, but it had instituted some additional applicant services. These consisted of job-finding workshops for the newly graduated, a self-service occupational library, and a series of handouts developed by the occupational analyst and reflecting immediate conditions on the market for various occupations. Counseling reflected the applicant load and continued to be concerned with the traditional counseling criteria, goals, and tools.

So far as the manager was concerned, the most significant and appreciated change in bureaucratic atmosphere was the consiedrable increase in managerial freedom. For the first time, she felt that she was actually making independent decisions. Manuals were largely ignored, and the management inspection team from Sacramento, which once made periodic visits to the office, had not been there for a considerable time.

Although the office staff meetings involved considerable feedback from the staff, the office could hardly be considered "free swinging." The staff consisted of about forty workers, just about the same number as were engaged in these activities in 1962. (Here, too, the staff increased in size during the years but had been cut back again.) The average age of the staff was 57 years. Only three members were under fifty. Most had been with the department for over ten years.

A revealing contrast can be made in that office between 1962 and 1970. In 1962 the number of placements made for each staff equivalent was 124, or 2.4 per week. In 1970, this figure had dropped to approximately 1.5 a week for each staff member.

The manager offered the observation that the same agency was housing two essentially separate agencies with conflicting needs. One focused on the problems of the disadvantaged applicant and had little concern with serving the needs of the employer. The other served all applicants and had a need to retain and cultivate the employer community.

The contrast between the two 1970 downtown offices and the degree to which they reflected their own labor markets suggests a series of basic questions that are applicable to the wider scene: Is a single model and a single mission for the employment service appropriate or even rational for all communities, all labor markets, and all occupations? Why has it not been possible to chart a particular market in terms of its true placement potential in order to determine the form of operation for a particular installation? Why do all evaluative instruments assume that all offices have the same labor exchange potential, depending only on population, without regard to the alternative job-matching mechanisms operating in that arena? Why does the Department of Labor continue to act as if there is only one national labor market in which all employment service offices have an equally valid placement role?

These are speculative questions, but they remain unaddressed.

Comparative View of the 1962 and 1970 Offices

Unfortunately, there are no ways to measure effectiveness but the traditional ones. And no matter how reluctant one is to apply them, the picture is unmistakably devastating and beyond rationalization (see Table 1). The one objective, dominating rationalization is the difference in unemployment rates. However one would wish to defend and applaud the efforts of the 1960s, and no matter how little credence is placed on recent ESARS statistics or the value of a placement figure, there is no way to escape the conclusion that the mission of the agency is in serious question. The proliferation of staff paralleled by the loss in local office activities statistics is overwhelming. Perhaps it is time to raise the fundamental question of whether simply adding staff *is* necessarily a resource. More doctors may indeed mean more and better health care for the sick. But it does not follow that more staff in the manpower field means more jobs or training programs for the public. In what ways, combinations, and levels can staff be considered a resource, and when does sheer size become more a deterrent than a resource?

It is true that 80 percent of the staff — almost all of the increase during the decade under study — was allocated specifically to operating programs for and providing services to disadvantaged persons. It is also true that much individualized service was performed which does not show in the statistics. If there was evidence that the personalized service was effective, then anyone

TABLE 1.

Comparison of Employment Service Activities

(1962-72)*

Category	Number†	
	1962	1972
Size of San Francisco work force	476,700	512,800
Size of employment service staff	83	383
Local placements	30,963	26,040
Average placements per month	2,584	2,127
New applications	78,800	54,339
Average new applications per month	6,567	4,528
Counseling cases	10,595	11,222
Average counseling cases per month	884	935

*Administrative changes occurred during this period which should be noted. First, in mid-1962 the industrial and service offices, which had been reporting separately, were combined. Second, the local office activities of the casual labor office were part of the reporting statistics of the industrial office. Third, the Youth Opportunity Center was established as a separate reporting entity in August 1962. Fourth, some offices were no longer operative by 1972, and some no longer dealt directly with the job-seeking public; e.g., the central order taking unit dealt only with the job orders taken from employers.

†All figures are fiscal year figures (1962 and 1972) except "size of San Francisco work force" and "size of employment service staff," which are calendar year figures for 1961 and 1971, respectively.

with social and humanistic concern can easily see the contrasts shown in the table, but unfortunately the evidence does not support this. It cannot be denied that there were fourteen more installations and three hundred more staff workers in 1972 than in 1962. To one degree or another they were all involved in putting the unemployed on jobs. The activities of all are reflected in the totals of local office activities, including WIN and CEP. It is true that the registration policy in 1972 was much less encompassing than it was in 1962. For example, in 1972 unemployment claims were considered registration for large numbers of union members and were therefore not counted; that was not true in 1962, when limited registration cards were required and counted. Nevertheless, it is also true that new registrations *were* being accepted at nine different points in 1972.

And while the registration policy was far looser in 1972 than in 1962, and more job seekers were able to come to the agency and examine the Job Information Centers without registering for work, it was also true that a far greater number of welfare clients and food stamp recipients were required to register for work in 1972 than in 1962. Vietnam veterans were also swelling registration ranks in 1972. In San Francisco there were some 40,000 more jobs in 1972 than there were in 1962, which meant that more job shifts occurred. And if one were to accept the fact that the agency moved toward a more personalized service, why is it that the counseling cases increased by such a small margin? Between 1965 and 1970 job openings placed in the employment service went down 42 percent statewide.

This picture is by no means unique to San Francisco. It can be duplicated in nearly every urban center in the country.

The conclusion is unmistakable. The agency is used less and less by both employers and job seekers. What is far less clear is why this is so. It is suggested here that the explanation does not lie primarily in the fact that the agency emphasized service to the disadvantaged during the 1960s. Nor does the solution lie in reversing that emphasis. It is suggested that the root causes are far more reflective of objective realities about the labor market and how it operates than they are the result of subjective evaluations of the agency or its own concepts of mission. It is the contention here that the options are no longer there. It does not matter whether the agency is "good" or "bad," or whether it pursues the job-matching model or the focus on serving the disadvantaged. Neither goal can be attained without massive changes at a basic level. Realistically, these are the wrong questions to ask, the wrong dichotomies to pose. They can only elicit the wrong answers.

Increased emphasis on placements may indeed increase the figures. If job turnovers in a given market are 10,000 a month, for example, and if the current placement of 1,000 a month is raised to 1,250 (a 25 percent increase), does that really validate the service and give it a respectable place in the universe of 10,000? And when those additional 250 placements are examined and prove to be dishwashers, materials handlers, and waitresses — jobs with minimal wage rates — does that really make the employment service look better? Shouldn't the question remain: For what market and for whose benefit does the employment service function? And suppose there is a sudden shortage of workers due to an economic boom or a national emergency. Suppose job orders pour into the employment service office because employers are searching everywhere for employees and using every tool at their command, including private employment agencies and the newspaper want ads. Suppose that in order to fill their needs the employers lower their specifications and hire almost everyone they can locate. If all those things happen and placement counts do indeed increase, will *those* statistics validate the agency?

The pressure is on in state and federal offices to prove the value of the agency by making more placements. Little is said these days about unemployment in the ghettos. In California there is continued lip service to the concept of serving the disadvantaged, because the Human Resources Development Act is still the law. But there is no way to interpret the present direction except as "coming full circle." To close the circle means that you go back to where you started — the 1962 office. That scene, that counter, that interviewer's moving finger, that exclusion, and that arrogance represent the present direction in the Labor Department and the California Department of Human Resources, no matter what the rhetoric and no matter what is intended by new and unknowledgeable administrators.

For those of us who were there, the grass was not that green.

THE
HAYWARD EXPERIMENT

No "counter" point examination of the employment service in California would be complete without a consideration of the Hayward experiment. Observers from throughout the state — and indeed from throughout the nation — looked to offices such as Hayward for possible solutions to some of the problems which had plagued the employment service almost since its inception.

Two themes are central to understanding the rationale behind the Hayward experiment: First, the primary goal was to provide a service to that segment of the employment service clientele which does not succeed in finding jobs through the local office. Although the size of this segment varies in different areas at different times, it is safe to say that it constitutes some 80 to 90 percent of employment service users. Second, whatever variety of conscious reason operated among whose who worked on the Hayward model, the underlying motivation was the opportunity to remove those elements that poisoned the air in the 1962 office. The experiment sought to rid the local office of every physical and procedural device that traditionally characterized the encounter between job seeker and bureacracy.

The Hayward experiment was *not* designed to increase placements. Despite the national rhetoric which was adopted, it was *not* designed to free staff members for intensive casework with the disadvantaged. In this instance at least the employment service office accepted its basic impotency, its incapacity to significantly alter its labor exchange role. It recognized its essential inability to change the world for the disadvantaged. The experiment was an attempt to put the office and whatever tools it could devise on the side of the people, not arrayed against them. It was an attempt to cross over the counter, to "open up." In a most profound and hopeful way, Hayward was a declaration of the bankruptcy of the past and of the inadequacy of existing models.

The central figure around whom the model was constructed was the least knowledgeable job seeker, the least aggressive applicant, the individual who had been most intimidated and ignored by the 1962 model — the disadvantaged person. And yet every experienced employment service person knows that the so-called "job ready" also experience discomfort when intimidated; they also have inadequate knowledge of the job world. They differ from the disadvantaged only in degree and in the resources they have to cope with their discomfort. The Hayward delivery system assumed that all people have a need to be treated decently, dealt with honestly, and helped if there is help to give.

The Hayward experiment set out to design and improve its own tools so that it *would* have something to give.

The planning of the project began in January 1970. The office became operational in August 1970. By December 1971 the experiment was extended to two additional offices. One was the San Francisco industrial and services office; the other was in Santa Rosa, a semirural community fifty miles north of San Francisco. By 1972 the project was fighting for its life. At the beginning of 1973 only traces of the experiment remained operative in the three offices, although many other offices had adopted various elements of the project.

It all began in December 1969 when the description of a proposed new model for a local office manpower delivery service appeared in the regional office of the Department of Human Resources Development. The proposed model originated at the Division of Manpower Administration in the Department of Labor. The model was in the process of being installed by the Department of Labor and a consulting firm in ten selected experimental local offices throughout the country. The paper describing the model was entitled "The Employment Service as a Comprehensive Manpower Agency," and the project came to be known nationally as COMO in acronymic reference to its designation as a "Conceptual Model."

In the eyes of the regional director and some of his staff, the proposal contained a major breakthrough, a chance to vitalize the agency and allow it to play a more relevant role for its users. And although the agency was assigning most of its resources for the disadvantaged to the central city offices, there was a great deal of concern with the kind of service available to the poor and the minorities who were not located in the city centers but in smaller communities. Many offices in small communities (as well as "regular" downtown offices) had been stripped of resources and staff to facilitate new operations under the Human Resources Development Act.

The regional director saw in the COMO proposal a loosened model which would permit an office a far wider range of alternatives and services than ever before officially envisioned. It projected a shift from maximum information gathering and record keeping activities to minimal paper work and maximum service.

Broadly defined, the COMO model described three groupings of applicant services: a self-directed job information service for the so-called "job ready," an employability exploration with job development service for those needing some help, and intensive employability development services for the seriously disadvantaged. The three tiers were based on a hierarchy of applicant needs. Resources were to be concentrated on the intensive employability development function, using a controlled case load based on the work incentive (WIN) team approach. The team approach meant that a small group of staff members, each with different specialties, worked on the problems of one applicant.

The COMO proposal directed that the installation of a computerized Job Bank in the local office was an essential prerequisite for participation in the project. At that time California was resisting the installation of the Job Bank. The regional office staff felt the Job Bank would not provide significant improvement over the Job Information Centers which had been installed in all northern California offices and which contained teletype machines to permit instant transmittal of job information among offices in a single labor market.

The regional director decided that the northern California regional office would conduct its own experiment in a selected local office. He recognized that the northern California agency already had considerably more innovative experience with providing services to the disadvantaged than any other group in the country, and he decided it was both unnecessary and undesirable to accept the design and installation from other sources. He felt the "experts" were within his jurisdiction.

In seeking ways to draw the agency's expertise into the experiment, the regional director established an advisory committee which consisted of a number of administrators from the area and such specialists as the chief of the research and statistics section. The advisory committee was to function somewhat as an in-house consulting firm. The local office manager of whichever office was selected for the experiment was to be included on the advisory committee.

That office turned out to be the one in the small city of Hayward, located thirty miles from San Francisco. There were a number of reasons for selecting Hayward. The city had a single office rather than multiple offices. It was a traditional office which had never varied from the manual model, and it was staffed mainly with long-time civil service employees, almost all of them white. The local office manager enthusiastically agreed to the experiment. (A resistant or disinterested manager would have made the effort impossible, especially given the atmosphere regarding decentralized management that was prevalent in the agency at that time.) The Hayward area was highly industrialized and had shown remarkable growth in recent years. Although it was affected by the recession, the area was not considered economically disadvantaged. The labor market was active, which would give the experiment at least some chance to be tested. Population in the area was primarily blue collar, with a small black community and a large population of Spanish-speaking citizens in and around the town. The office was the only employment service installation in southern Alameda County, serving a population of nearly five hundred thousand in ten cities.

The agency was housed with the unemployment insurance program in a large, extremely busy office. The public lobby was always filled with long lines of insurance claimants. The employment service staff sat on one side of the office at rows of desks behind the inevitable counter. There was a small, insignificant job information center in a corner of the vast lobby. It displayed a limited number of job listings.

The conceptual model tentatively developed by the regional office was a variation of the COMO model. The Hayward experiment developed independently from the Department of Labor's COMO experiment, and information and experiences were not exchanged between the two on a regular basis. The models differed primarily in that the Hayward model placed far less emphasis on the categorization of the applicants into three tiers. Also, Hayward laid considerably more stress on the second tier in the hierarchy of services, that one which dealt with employability exploration and job development. The self-service job information center (the first tier of the COMO proposal) was already somewhat operative in the Hayward office and would require little effort to enlarge and improve. The COMO third tier, that of casework intensive services, was simply incorporated intact from the COMO model, but it did not represent a significant change in office operations, and it was not of special interest to the experimenters.

The overall goal of the project was:

> To demonstrate a method for the delivery of manpower services which is focused on responsiveness to the needs of the individual job seeker, *as he perceives them,* and which undertakes to provide him with access to the job market.[1]

It was agreed that the activities of the office would be consistently held to the following operating principles:

(1) The obligation of the project to the public consists of providing a service whereby every job seeker who uses it spends his time productively while in the office and gains something of value for himself in competing for a job.

(2) The project accepts the value of self-help as a desirable way to relate to the public. It accepts the concept that people have the right and capacity to make choices

---

[1] Hayward Project Advisory Committee, "Goals and Operating Principles — Hayward Project," unpublished report, March, 1970.

about their needs if they are given the knowledge and the options.

(3) It adheres to a policy of openly sharing all the resources it has and acknowledging what it hasn't in its dealings with the public.

(4) The project is committed to creating an atmosphere that seeks to reduce public anxiety, fear, and apprehension association with the search for work, which includes contact with the public employment service.

(5) The goals and objectives are best served by developing the project with staff participation and by continuously fostering the creative capacities of the staff.

(6) The project operates on the principle that it will continuously evaluate the effectiveness of its own activities in terms of the project goals and principles and will develop and maintain flexibility and a capacity to make changes and adjustments.[2]

A proposed model was prepared for the regional office by the author, at that time functioning as a consultant to the regional director. The model was contained in a paper titled "Variations on a Theme."[3] Some of the services and processes proposed in the model were subsequently rejected by the local office or the advisory committee as unworkable or too costly, but the proposal provided a working skeleton and much of the rationale for the experiment as it finally developed. One section of the document contained a tabular comparison of the proposed model with the traditional model. It was called "Contrasts":

It might be well to contrast the underlying attitudes, philosophies, practices, and activities of this model with a standard employment service office. This is not intended to imply that in those offices there are not individual interviewers and counselors who make heroic and sometimes successful efforts to break through the built-in premises. Nevertheless, this is an attempt to contrast the basic operations of the two models.

---

2 *Ibid.*
3 Miriam Johnson, "Variations on a Theme," unpublished report, 1970.

Regular Office	This Model
The central purpose of the office is to refer job seekers to listed job openings.	The central purpose is to equip the job seeker with all available knowledge, tools, advice, and information that will enable him to better manipulate the market. This includes referring job seekers to listed job openings.
A major activity is **obtaining** information **from** an applicant.	The major activity is gathering and **giving** pertinent information **to** the applicant.
A person is processed and assessed before services are performed. The office determines what the person should have access to.	Providing services to the job-seeking public is direct. People aren't processed — only paper is. Job seekers use whatever services they want or need.
Most pertinent job information is for the use of the staff and is closed to the public, except as staff is asked or as time permits.	All information and knowledge is shared with the public, openly, and is provided in every form: visually, by written material, orally, etc. Only that which is forbidden by law is suppressed.
Unless he has a job referral, a person can come in again and again, wait, spend time, and walk out with nothing more than he had when he came in, except that he is weakened, exasperated, and feeling less adequate. He has gained nothing; he has only lost.	With or without a job referral, a person can obtain a list of places to look for work, information about employers in the local market, improved interviewing techniques, and information about training and occupations in the local market. All of the time the person has spent has been directly productive to him.
Even with a job referral, the job seeker may not get the job because of bad interviewing techniques or an inadequate application.	This model focuses the job seeker's attention on the possibility that he may be harming his own opportunities, and it provides corrective devices.

Regular Office	This Model
The physical arrangements and processes are designed for the comfort and convenience of the agency and staff.	A public office should be designed for the convenience of the public. Staff adapts its working methods to that primary consideration.
The major portion of staff time is used to satisfy the demands of the agency: recording transactions, writeups, taking lengthy work applications that are never used, scheduling procedures, and supervision.	The major portion of staff time is devoted to activity that is of direct and immediate value in helping the job seeker. Agency needs are reduced to a bare minimum. Information taking is reduced to strictly need-to-know information.
The paraphernalia of the put-down prevails. Counters, desks, waiting lines, and waiting sections affect people negatively. They constitute clear symbols of the authority - subservient roles. They are intimidating. They increase distance between staff and client. They make the encounter dehumanized and impersonal.	Physical layout and places for communicating are designed to equalize the encounter and humanize the service. The psychological effect is supportive. The bureaucratic processes which are of value to the agency are physically separated from the services and hardware which are of value to the public.
If the office fails to provide a job, it appears in the eyes of the public and the job seeker to have failed to perform its function and to be implicitly dishonest.	The office can give exactly what it promises to everyone —access to all the jobs it **has** and all the expertise it has to help a job seeker find his own. It does not claim to do what it can't do.
Services are conceived as "doing things for people."	Services are conceived as helping people do things for themselves by equipping them with the best available tools.
The staff develops feelings of frustration, fraudulence, and apathy because so little of their work bears fruit.	Staff is continuously engaged in giving what it has, directly. Staff is encouraged to use its creative resources.

Regular Office	This Model
A small percentage of applicants get very good, individualized service from those few interviewers who spend much time developing jobs. Some interviewers have highly developed relationships with groups of employers.	Unless ample staff is provided, this model may cause a loss of this type of service. This is unfortunate. It would be good to try to preserve it. However, this model will provide help to far more people.

It was the intent of the regional office to change the job duties and retrain the professional staff so that a "placement officer" or "counselor" would become a "labor market consultant" who would provide consultive *and* placement services to the job seeker and to the employer. The term "consultant" seemed particularly fitting since the use of a consultant is determined by the wishes of the user rather than the procedures of a bureaucracy.

The office was to become an information and educational center, with the ability to provide the public with a full range of occupational and job search information in order to increase the job seeker's ability to get and hold a job as well as to make occupational choices. To accomplish this required that the staff itself develop a far greater knowledge base than it previously possessed.

Staff training concentrated on developing the capacity of the staff to identify problems and sharpening knowledge about the most effective way to help individuals with a variety of problems in looking for work. Training also included steps to help the staff develop a better knowledge of their own market. This was accomplished by two training methods. First, staff members in groups of three or four participated for a full week in workshops with job seekers. The workshops were conducted by experienced workshop leaders provided by the regional office. The problems raised by the public participants were the raw material from which the staff developed its understanding about the search for work. Second, the staff participated in developing an occupational data bank under the guidance of the staff from the regional research and statistics unit.

The Hayward staff initially exhibited considerable resistance to the magnitude of the proposed change. Most of the staff members had been in the agency a long time, and they were distrustful.

They were mindful of the shifts of bureaucratic mandates and were fearful that they would be so left "out on the limb," out of accord with the national design. And so, despite the apparent approval and support of the immediate hierarchy, there was a great deal of trepidation on the part of the front-line staff. In the last analysis, the intuitive understanding they had of the bureaucratic and political processes proved them right. In a sense, they were indeed betrayed. Such experiences, repeated over many years, help explain the mediocrity and conformity of many bureaucratic organizations. Staff members learn not to take chances.

However, as the project took shape, as old constraints surfaced and were reexamined, and as the staff became involved in developing the design and resources, the resistance in most cases turned to support. Soon after the experiment began operating, even the most skeptical staff members and even those most committed to the standard job-matching operation agreed that all the employers were getting faster action on their orders than they ever did under the former system.

The severity of the recession which occurred at about the same time as the Hayward experiment went into effect made a simple comparison of placement statistics impossible, but it was clear the fear that employers would discontinue the use of the service was unwarranted. All of the staff agreed that the public was continually delighted with the changed office. This approval was demonstrated verbally and statistically. The experiment began simultaneously with the separation of the employment service from the unemployment insurance function. The office moved to a new location some two miles away where a Youth Opportunity Center was already in operation. It had previously been assumed that the greatest flow of traffic to the employment service came from unemployment insurance claimants, and it was only logical to anticipate that moving to a new location would result in a severe drop in traffic, at least for a time. Apparently this did not occur. From 120 to 200 persons came to the office daily.

The office became fully operational by August 1970. The opening had an immediate and almost magical effect. The new procedures appealed to everyone — the regional office staff, the public users, and the hundreds of visitors from schools, the federal government, other states, and other local offices and regions within

California. This last group was significant, because of the hundred or so California Department of Human Resources Development employees who came to visit, most were front-line interviewers and supervisors. No other group examined the office with a more critical and knowledgeable eye than the local office people. Their reactions were overwhelmingly enthusiastic. It was difficult to imagine that such wide staff exposure and acceptance would not influence the direction of the agency. It did, in fact, influence many local offices which adapted various aspects of the Hayward experiment to their own office operations, but it apparently had little influence on the general direction of the agency.

Much thought went into the physical aspects of the office, as the operating principles would suggest. The building was remodeled so that a wall was placed between the area where the public had access to all that it saw — the Job Information Center — and that part which need not be visible to the flow of traffic — the agency office in which clerical activities and interviews by appointment were conducted. For administrative purposes, the employees in the public part were called the "Job Information Center unit," and the agency part which included the management staff were called the "employability development unit." The public office itself housed two kinds of activities in separated sections — job openings and job search.

A person looking for work first went through the job opening section. What met his eye was a large wall of colorful bulletin boards, kiosks, and stands. Job orders — cellophane wrapped — hung under prominently displayed occupational headings. Chairs were provided around a table. Current civil service openings were arranged by occupations and types of services and bound into books. The books were on the table near pencils and paper. The veterans bulletin board described the services for veterans. A special services bulletin board announced the services available for low-income people; qualifying income levels were given for both national and state programs. An out-of-town bulletin board displayed the inventory of job orders, overseas jobs, and jobs in Alaska. The community bulletin board displayed listings of community agencies dealing with social problems and the services they provided. A job-finding workshop poster announced this daily local office activity and described its value. All of the public displays of information were either new or revised to make them more valuable and explicit for the job seeker.

On each bulletin board the individual was advised that the services existed, who was eligible for them, and how they might be obtained. The choice was left to the job seeker. An audiovisual program was designed by the office to perform this orientation function. The script included instructions to the public about how to interpret a job order and how to screen and evaluate themselves. Unfortunately, funds to install this device were never granted.

Needless to say, there was no counter. Instead of a counter and a reception line, a staff member wearing a name tag and called a "greeter" came to the job seeker and asked if he needed help and understood how to use the office. Many questions that would ordinarily be asked at the reception counter were quickly disposed of. The job opening section was in constant use. Chairs were arranged around tables to spare clients the isolation and awkwardness of sitting in rows waiting to be called. Visitors sat around the tables, chatted, read, wrote out referral slips, took notes from civil service listings, and talked to each other and the greeters.

A person who could not find a job that interested him on the board was invited to go to the adjoining public office if he wished to learn more about looking for work.

There were a few interview desks in both of the two public sections. They were arranged unobtrusively along the side or in back of the area.

A large sign hanging in the middle of the second public section announced "Job Search Services." A short counter along the side of the room was used as a place for applicants to bring their job selection slips and arrange appointments with job search interviewers. Any person could walk up to any of the designated areas and ask anyone visible for help.

The visual displays in the job search section were:

Job Leads Board — On this board were selected newspaper advertisements, typed notices about various companies and industries which might be hiring, laying off, or opening new establishments, seasonal notices, and other types of information. A staff member had the responsibility for keeping the board current and pertinent, but the public was invited to add information to the board. The staff was counted on to verify the accuracy of this information. This was an experimental innovation developed by the staff.

Industries Map — On this large, impressive map of the area were tiny flags indicating the location of 150 to 200 major firms, together with public transportation information. This was also an innovation developed by the staff.

Pamphlet Racks — These contained the job search mini-guides developed by the regional research and statistics section. They were printed in Spanish and English. There was also national Youth Corps and Job Corps information and handouts from the Fair Employment Practices Commission. These had been available before but were displayed more prominently and attractively in the Hayward office.

Career Information — This display was changed at regular intervals. The display might concentrate on health occupations for a time, and then be changed to data processing occupations. This was an innovation contributed by the librarian.

The occupational library was housed in the job services area. It became the busiest section in job search, increasingly used by both staff and public. It contained the sum total of all occupational, industrial, employer, union, and labor market information that could be assembled. An employer directory was included. In the center was a manned desk, with a staff member or librarian servicing both staff and public. Around the desk was a comfortable reading and writing area with furniture arranged to resemble a public library. The position of librarian or "labor market information coordinator" was a new job developed for the Hayward project. The main responsibility was to develop and maintain the labor market information system in the office. Many offices in northern California later designated similar positions.

An interesting insight into the dynamics of the experiment is provided by examining the evolution of the occupational library. Originally, there was a library developed for the public and a different library at the rear for the staff. Inevitably, it became obvious that what the staff needed to know was exactly what the public wanted to know, and so the two libraries were combined into one and located in the public section.

The delivery system of the office was basically opposed to one which required that everyone be processed in an identical fashion. The model conceived of publicly offering a series of services which clients could reject or select, as they chose. The concept was intended to emulate that of a marketplace or a travel agency. The services or wares were displayed, and there were well-equipped experts to assist or advise. Staff could be shifted depending upon flow and need.

Services Offered by the Hayward Office

The range of services offered and functions performed by the Hayward office at its most viable point included:

Placements — A centralized order-taking unit conducted all dealings with employers and controlled the display of jobs in the Job Information Center. Job development activities were performed by any member of the staff who saw the opportunity to do so. File search was regularly conducted by the veterans employment representative and was periodically conducted by other staff members when jobs were not being filled by the flow of traffic.

The state policy on applicant registrations was unclear at that time, since the state was then engaged in a conflict with the Department of Labor over the introduction of the Employment Service Activities Reporting System (ESARS) into California. The very essence of the Hayward project was in conflict with enforced registration and excessive paperwork. Applications were taken for anyone who identified himself as a Vietnam veteran, a Human Resources Development client, a Job Corps returnee, or a welfare client referred by the welfare office. Anyone who wished to do so was free to leave an application card. However, the office made it clear that the search of files was not the primary method for matching, that all jobs went on the board, and that none were retained for the registered applicants. Those people with good skills for whom a job was not apt to come in often were asked to leave an application card or a self-addressed interest card describing their qualifications. They were assured that the card would be mailed back to them if a job in their occupation was listed. A physical count of users was made by the office at regular intervals.

(The original design of the office had projected the issuance of a card similar to a credit card which would provide a data gathering and tracking system. This would have involved the staff in a minimum of paper work, most of which could have been handled by clerks. But the threat of the ESARS system and the possible conflict with forms required by ESARS if it came into effect made investment in these cards unwise.)

Employer Relations — The office invited groups of employers to the office for tours and for participation in the daily workshops. Very little direct employer visiting was performed.

Veterans Employment Services — Although this had been an ongoing service, it was considerably more active because Vietnam veterans were returning in large numbers. As a consequence of the project, the veterans employment representative developed workshops for groups of veterans.

Manpower Training Programs — The service provided both information and processing for all funded manpower training programs. This service was essentially unchanged by the project.

Domestic Placement Service — A half-time interviewer ran a domestic placement desk. This was unchanged by the project.

Outreach Services — this consisted of two staff members who carried traditional employment service activities into outlying cities on a scheduled rotational basis. This too was unchanged by the project.

Employability Development Team — Although the team was installed as a consequence of the project, it had not been an integral part of the original project design. The team was manned by former Youth Opportunity Center counselors. Intended for disadvantaged minorities, the team continued to have a case load of young persons brought over by the counselors when the offices were combined. The occupational library, the data bank, and the community resources file developed by the project became useful tools for the employability development team, as they did for all other programs. The employability development team was located in the agency side of the office and functioned only by appointment and referral. It operated on a limited case-load basis.

Job Search Services — This was the most important new service offered by the experiment, and it was the heart of the experiment. It consisted of the occupational library, the data bank, three job search interviewers, and a counselor. Job seekers who were unable to find a suitable opening from the open orders availed themselves of this service. The interviewers reviewed the needs of the applicant, selected the appropriate material from the data bank and occupational library, and assisted the applicant in developing a list of appropriate employers, unions, or other job-matching mechanisms to contact for work. The interviewer and the applicant discussed the most desirable job-interviewing technique for that particular applicant in his particular occupation and in relation to particular employers. The most effective method of completing the employer's work application was also reviewed. The total activity provided the applicant with a job search plan. Job search interviewers also referred applicants who needed and wanted more counseling or assistance to the employability development team or to whatever other service was indicated. If in the course of discussion the job search interviewer saw the opportunity to call an employer on behalf of the applicant, he did so. Often the discussion involved considering occupational decisions for which the occupational library was a good reference tool.

Workshops — This was a daily scheduled activity conducted for an hour or two with members of the public who cared to participate. It centered on the various problems most often encountered in confronting the marketplace, including fear and depression. The entire group engaged in an effort to solve the difficulties of various participants and to respond to mock interview situations. They provided each other with leads and advice. Although workshops were disruptive to office routine, the participants invariably emerged less fearful, more informed, and sincerely grateful for the encounter. The workshops provided the staff with an excellent listening device from which to get frank expressions of reaction to the experiment and from which to form perceptions about needs.

Community Resources File — A file on rollers contained the full array of community information that had always before resided in the heads of counselors or on their various desks. The file included information about a methadone program, resources for obtaining free dental work, planned parenthood information, the telephone number of Alcoholics Anonymous, and all other information about resources available in the area for every type of social, personal, or medical problem that was apt to be encountered. The file was developed by the staff and was a useful tool to every staff member at whatever station.

Staff Responsibilities

The public side of the office had fifteen staff persons, two of whom were supervisors, and the half-time domestic placement interviewer. This meant that thirteen staff members had to deal with the public, run the workshops, and maintain the labor market information system. In order to accomplish this, the staff had to be free of agency demands for written paper work that was not immediately productive. One of the conditions that was laid down when the project began was that no additional staff would be provided. The experiment had to be conducted using only the normal staff complement. To ensure that staff activities were as flexible and interchangeable as possible, a rotation system was devised between the job search interviewers, the greeters, and the referral interviewers so that roles could be shifted as the need indicated.

Depending on flow of traffic, there were one to three greeters who introduced themselves to individuals or groups, offered assistance, interpreted the job orders, accepted interest cards, helped individuals make out referral slips for the jobs they had selected, answered questions, and made appointments for other services within the office. The greeter was particularly alert to those visitors who had an obvious reading problem, who looked troubled or puzzled, or who appeared to lack the aggressiveness to express their needs. Anyone seen leaving the office without a job referral was approached, and job search services were offered. Usually one of the greeters was Spanish-speaking. All wore name tags, but they were otherwise indistinguishable from the public as they stood or sat alongside the job seekers.

One to three interviewers handled the job referrals, depending on demand. The interviewers reviewed the orders selected to be sure that they were clearly understood and discouraged inappropriate job choices. The office experimented with a total "no screening" policy, but abandoned it because of employer reaction and because it was felt by the staff to be in violation of an operating principle of the project — the sharing of all knowledge with the public. Thus, if an interviewer knew that a particular company had a rigid policy against hiring long-haired men, the interviewer felt dishonest if he failed to inform long-haired applicants of this. The final decision about whether to apply for a job was left to the job seeker. However, in a study conducted by the office, it was found that interpretation of the order, discussion, and explanation by the referral interviewer circumvented referrals to inappropriate jobs selected by applicants about a third of the time. This was always by mutual agreement, never by authoritarian direction. Any member of the staff was free to make a referral, subject to the control of the central order-taking unit.

The occupational data bank became the single most important piece of hardware in the entire office, and it was most essential to the Hayward concept. There is no substantial way to help a person look for work unless there is a body of pertinent information about employers to tap. One interviewer in Hayward described it in this way: "Before, if someone asked where they should go to look for work, I'd have to rack my brain and finish up with the yellow pages of the phone book or the same few employers I knew. Now, I go to the data bank, pull the person's occupation, and I know I've got every company there that ever gave us an order and every bit of knowledge that anyone in the office ever had about that occupation."

Arranged by occupational codes and cross-filed in usable family groups, all inactive orders received by the office during the previous years were contained in the bank. The orders were continually updated, corrected, and modified. Current orders were placed in the data bank as they became inactive. Staff members were thoroughly debriefed about their knowledge of each occupation in the Hayward area, and the information was stored in the data bank. The information concerned employers' hiring practices, union relationships, training requirements, and all training facilities. Everything the interviewer learned was put immediately into usable and retrievable form. When all the bits and pieces were assembled, occupations were evaluated to determine the significant gaps in information. The office then set about contacting employers, unions, and agencies to obtain the missing data and interfile it. "Ticklers" were established which listed groups of employers in relation to the problems of particular groups of job seekers — for instance, employers who hired women production workers, employers who hired male clerical workers, companies which had indicated a willingness to hire the handicapped or older workers or veterans, companies willing to train, companies that hired part-time help or worked a night shift, and so on. The "ticklers" extracted specialized information from the job orders which would otherwise have been lost in the body of the file. The sorting, extracting, and filing was done by hand and involved the whole staff.

The value of the inactive job orders to the job seekers and interviewers raises some intriguing questions about the national computerized Job Banks. The wide gap between how front-line staff perceives a need and what administrators see as needs become apparent when looking at the information systems each designed. The Job Banks are designed to provide the public with access to the jobs which are currently open, to provide administrators with evaluative data, and to provide researchers, statisticians, and program planners with insights into wage data, future training needs, migration information, and evaluation information. On the other hand, the field staff recognized the great value of the job order to that large body of individuals who do *not* get placed by the open order. Under their design the interviewer, who was really the agent or advocate for this large group of unplaced individuals, used essentially the same data base as the computerized Job Banks except that the data were stored and made retrievable for assistance to both staff and public. The data were important for job search purposes and for other local office service needs. It is significant that such a use for the data did not occur to Job Bank planners and administrators.

The principle that the public has the right to use or approach anything or anyone it can see was slightly modified in the case of the "tubs" containing the data bank. A staff member pulled out the appropriate occupational group for a job seeker, and the job seeker, with the advice and help of the interviewer, reviewed the cards and selected the companies he wanted to contact. Since a job order contained information most pertinent to him — such as wages, shifts, skill level, and qualities desired — he was able to make some knowledgeable selections about where to concentrate his search. If the interviewer determined that the reading ability or comprehension of the person was inadequate for the task, the interviewer prepared the job search plan. This procedure was in keeping with the self-help principle enunciated by the project. The staff was exhorted to be rigidly honest in warning the person that the office had *no* knowledge that the company actually had an opening or that the information about the company was current. The job seeker was asked to assist the office and other applicants by feeding back new information about the company that might be helpful to the next person. The person was plainly told that the office did not have the staff or resources to keep these data current without help from the public.

As the office became operational, many omissions, oversights, and serious problems emerged. Some were of a practical nature, but others reflected how profound the change really was in all of its ramifications. Such things as the failure to fund the audiovisual device for orientation purposes resulted in an undue strain on the greeters as they found themselves taking too much time explaining repeatedly how the new office worked. Unfortunately, too many people were bypassed. The audiovisual device would have helped solve the problem, and it was ominous that the minimal costs involved in establishing such an essential device were withheld. A more critical omission was the absence of a conscientious public reeducation program directed to both job seekers and to the employers, using the full range of media. If a public service is going to be changed, the public should be informed in order to close the gap between public expectations and actual performance. Both employers and job seekers had years of experience with a particular kind of employment office, and they anticipated a standard, traditional agency when they walked in or phoned. The failure to conduct a public reeducation campaign and the absence of an audiovisual device placed an unnecessary burden on the staff.

(Apparently, these same problems were also encountered by the COMO offices.)

It would also seem that there are more vigorous and effective ways to bring the office to the attention of the employers to induce them to place their orders than the traditional employer visiting programs. The Hayward office had a basis for a new approach because it had a new experimental program to announce which was both newsworthy and interesting. A few groups of employers did visit the office, and it was clear that their reactions were generally positive. But this was far short of developing a basic approach, a sustained campaign, and a new kind of relationship with the employer community.

Serious flaws emerged in the model with regard to supervisory and management roles. Although the supervisory-staff relationship became less authoritarian, the removal of the traditional routine and the traditional document check left the supervisors with ill-defined functions. The office did not establish a satisfactory set of standards and operational checkpoints for the supervisors. It became evident that a different kind of leadership was needed if the project was to live up to its principle of continuous self-evaluation and responsiveness to needs. The operating principles called for a dynamic operation, not one frozen into routine. Support of that kind of dynamism required creative leadership.

The existence of the employability development team and its relationship to the experiment brought to the surface other problems which had wider implications than simply the effects upon the Hayward experiment. The office management was not able to set policy for the office, and particularly not for the employability development team. The standards prevailing at that time insisted that policy making be decentralized and that managers should manage. However, there had veen very little tradition in the employment service for decentralized policy making, and there had been little thought given to the development of policy-making capability. At the same time, there was never any real definition of what kinds of policy were within the rights of the manager to make. For example, the case load of the employability development team in Hayward was filled with strung-out, drug-ridden youth carried over from the Youth Opportunity Center. But the office was located in an area of high unemployment among a large contingent of Spanish-speaking people. Management should have been given the prerogative to determine which of the two population groups would be the recipient of the bulk of the limited resources available to the office. Then it would have been possible to pursue that target aggressively. The existence of poverty criteria for selection of the target population offered no help. The dropout, middle class youth could very well fall within those criteria, and a Mexican father of four could fall outside them because he earned slightly more than the established income level.

Another problem area surfaced in Hayward which raised serious questions about the language and definitions in manpower rhetoric. For the first time employment service personnel were talking to people in the lobby in an unstructured situation. It related to the term "job readiness" and its fuzzy implications. In an informal survey greeters were asked to describe what they considered a "job-ready person" and what kind of persons they tended to send to counselors for possible inclusion in the employability development team load. Their answers were enlightening. The openness of the question, "How can I help you?" and the range of responses changed the staff's perceptions of the clients. The greeters considered a person job ready if he could work, had worked, and wanted to work. They did not consider him nonready because of the condition of the market, or because the person had low skills. The basis of the judgment was not merely the fact that employers at that point did not need or want the person. The assessment actually was based on how the person appeared, how rational he seemed, and what kind of help he asked for. As a result, the people who were being sent to the counselors and eventually to the employability development team were those visibly unable to work except through excessive manipulations of the person or the market — mental retardees, the emotionally disturbed, those with drug or alcohol involvement, or those who had severe physical handicaps.

It is difficult to reconcile such selections with the definitions in the Human Resources Development Act of the person for whom the act was intended — those who were "employable or capable of being made employable through the services available under this part." One would have to believe that the services of the two young counselors constituted that which could make such people "employable or capable of being employed." And yet the greeters intuitively felt themselves incapable of considering someone less than employable on any basis other than what the job seeker said about himself. In a structured situation, the person doing the assessment would place an individual in the non-job-ready status by using criteria established by someone not involved in the person-to-person encounter.

There is a failure in all manpower efforts to define the difference between diagnosing a problem and treating it. The question of whether any employment service staff member has the skills or the resources to "treat" a series of personal problems of such magnitude as to defy the professionals has been begged not only by the Hayward office but by policy makers and administrators of manpower programs throughout the land. Although there has been lip service given to the fact that the staff is not equipped to cure a drug addict or an alcoholic, there has nevertheless been an absence of clear policy about what the front-line staff should do with such individuals. It was (and is) unclear *what* treatment actually is and what should be expected of counselors in dealing with such problems. This has resulted in de facto approval of the "treatment" orientation. It is an unproven premise indeed that the activities of a counselor or an employability development team have any direct influence on making a person "employable," whatever that is.

In all phases of the manpower effort there has been a continuing weakness in conceptualizing and describing the target population. The use of income criteria, of residence criteria, of terms such as "job readiness," "employable," and even such plain words as "employed" and "unemployed" have failed to impart operationally useful concepts to front-line staff. The concepts have always been inadequate for equipping the staff to be able to make essential distinctions between a middle-class youth playing at poverty, a ghetto program "hustler," and a black man locked into an unskilled occupation in the secondary labor market who is employed today and off tomororw but needs a tool — whether it is a job or training — with which to pry open the door to a future.

Some of the problems which were brought out by the Hayward experiment are endemic to the entire employment service. For example, staff attitude changes occurred to some degree, but the internalized bureaucratic axioms and modes tended to hang on. It was hard to give up the "know-all, have-all" air and replace it with honest admissions to the job seeker about office capabilities and inadequacies. "Honesty" was not the most precise word to use in describing the traditional way of dealing with the public, and many staff members seemed unable to acquire a capacity for it.

Despite the problems, during most of 1971 the experiment was regarded by the regional office as a successful effort worthy of export. Mindful of the dangers of wholesale export by fiat, the advisory committee and the regional staff sought a method for enlarging the experiment without destroying its vitality. The history of manpower programs is studded with examples of one successful effort in one community becoming the basis for a national program, and in that process becoming distorted and lifeless. The decision was made to include the two additional offices — San Francisco industrial and services and Santa Rosa — and the work proceeded.

Although the regional office was unreservedly enthusiastic about the Hayward experiment and the staff was convinced the approach offered clear value to the job seeker, it was felt that an objective evaluation was necessary. There was also recognition that the agency itself did not contain within it the kind of experience or capability necessary to conduct a thorough evaluation, since none of the traditional measurements were applicable. A prospectus was developed describing the experiment and requesting that the regional office of the Department of Labor provide the funds to contract with an outside consulting firm to conduct an evaluative study and to develop evaluative tools and methods for use by the agency.

There was no doubting the feeling in the Hayward office that the experiment was a success. This sense of success was part of the atmosphere that pervaded the office. It bore little resemblance to the 1962 office or even a typical 1970 employment service installation. People were busy. Staff and clients were reading, talking, writing, and looking at materials. There were no silent rows of grim-faced human beings sitting and waiting endlessly to be called. The counter and all its implications had been transcended. The staff was on its feet, in the lobby, sitting alongside . . . available. The impression was that interviewer and client were working *together*, pitting themselves against the problem, pursuing the elusive job, probing the market for the soft spot that would yield. All that the office knew and all that it had was visible and available to the public. It definitely appeared that the Hayward experiment was fulfilling its first principle: "Provide a service whereby every job seeker that uses it spends his time productively and gains something of value to himself in competing for a job."

Perhaps the most important reason behind the staff's enthusiasm was the reduced gap between implied promise and actual performance. Workers went home less tired, even though the processes in the office were far less orderly. Most interviewers involved in the daily grind of a regular office, where application taking and record keeping were main activities, suffered from a constant, nagging sense of fraudulence. They were assailed by doubts about the value of their activities. They were aware of the wide gap between what they actually did for most job seekers and the implied promises of the application card, the job order, the *Dictionary of Occupational Codes*, and the impressive desks. At the Hayward office it was a great relief for those experienced employees to be able to do for the job seeker exactly what was promised. The interviewer was able to help a man make a decision about going out on an open job order. No orders were hidden. The interviewer could help a person make a more productive kind of job search, and he had the tools with which to do it. The tools may not have been adequate — certainly no one claimed infallability — but the interviewer could offer the best cumulative experience of the agency and its staff. And it was a considerable offering. He could accomplish something with every person he saw, something honest and straight.

The relationship of staff to each other and to supervisors reflected these changes. The cross-fertilization of Youth Opportunity Center staff and regular office staff and the rotation of staff members was fruitful. The participation with the research and statistics consultants in developing the occupational data bank had considerably widened the tunnel through which the staff viewed the Hayward labor market. The staff was visibly more self-generating, self-policing, and participatory. It was evident during staff meetings, in the lunch room, and on the floor.

The most sustaining source of encouragement to the staff was the public. When asked to define the changes, a staff member wrote: "Job gratification in the past depended on performing unmeasurable services approved by the public."

That statement, in its brevity, captures the essence of the Hayward attempt. There was an unending stream of compliments, positive comments, and surprised reactions from users and visitors. Employment service staffs throughout the country develop thickened skins in order to withstand the public apathy, at best, and often its overt hostility. Letters of complaint are often written to legislators and administrators; the office always gets a copy. Contrast that with the impact on the office of letters such as:

> Dear Sir: I realize that you are a very busy man so will be brief. I wasn't in your office over five minutes when a person with a name of . . . on his lapel greeted me. He was most courteous and helpful. I observed others were being treated in the same manner. My morale was much higher when I left than when I came in. The very atmosphere in your office is such a man doesn't feel like an outcast human being, looking for something for nothing. I am sending a letter to the Governor of the treatment I have received in your office of the State Employment. Thank you.

There was definitely a feeling of optimism in the office, a feeling of success and accomplishment.

In 1971 an independent research firm made a study of manpower programs in four major U. S. cities. The San Francisco Bay Area was included, and of course the Hayward experiment became a part of the study. The final report described the Hayward project in what would prove to be ominous tones:

> Whether the Hayward experiment will be the path of the agency in the future depends on innumerable state and national decisions and directions that transcend the intent of the Regional Office. . . . The Hayward project will solve its problems and come to full maturity as a pioneering effort in public service *only* if it is assiduously protected and guarded from encroachment and erosions from any sources that might deflect its basic commitments. The Employment Service in Northern California has seen this happen before. There is little doubt that, compared to the 1960 office, the

Hayward experiment represents an upheaval of profound dimensions that transcends the simple overlay of new programs on unchanging structures. At least the local office has attempted to change itself as an institution.[4]

The encroachment and erosions were not long in making themselves felt. The experiment began to stumble in November 1971 when the regional director, who had been the major source of official agency approval for the Hayward experiment, was removed from his position as part of a total reorganization of the agency. He was placed in a role unrelated to line activity. Members of the advisory committee were also shifted to new posts, and since the committee had no official bureaucratic authorization, it was effectively dismantled. Soon no one remained who had responsibility for the Hayward experiment. And what was worse, no one remained to protect the Hayward project from the inevitable pressures to erode the base on which it was idealistically constructed. It was "nobody's job."

One such pressure occurred in January 1972. On the first working day of the year, every local office in the state of California, including the Hayward office, was required to participate fully in the ESARS record-keeping system. Until then, ESARS had been partially installed. An effort had been made to except Hayward from ESARS participation, but it failed. This meant that an ESARS I form with identifying information was required for every person walking into the office for whom a service was provided. Simultaneously, the registration policy was tightened and compulsory registration was instituted for an increasing flow of welfare recipients, for a sharp increase in Vietnam veterans, for all food stamp recipients, and for all poverty defined applicants. This amounted to over 50 percent of the applicant flow. The ESARS I form was an additional form to the application card, and so it meant that two forms had to be completed for half the individuals who came in the door.

An ESARS III form was required for every service performed by a staff member for an applicant. This form provided checks for all the services considered valid and countable for a

---

4 Olympus Research Corporation, "The Total Impact of Manpower Programs: A Four-City Case Study," unpublished report prepared for the U. S. Department of Labor, Washington, D. C., August, 1971, pp. 18-35, 36.

local office. It was enlightening to read the "acceptable" list. The specific activities listed were: orientation, counseling, job development, follow-up, and referral to supportive services, including health, welfare, rehabilitation, remedial education, and testing. All activities surrounding the placement process were reported by other devices. Registration was reported by the ESARS I form.

Each of the countable services was defined in instructional documents, and the conditions that had to prevail were detailed. To receive credit for providing orientation, the activity had to go on for two full days. To be able to check "group counseling," a counselor had to conduct the group. Not a single activity included in the Hayward experiment was countable — not the development or use of the data bank, not the occupational library, not the job search services, not the workshops (which were not conducted by counselors), not the greeter . . . nothing.

The office was suddenly inundated by useless paper work. The flood of required registrations was considered by the staff to be completely unproductive, since all the jobs were listed on the board. Staff members had developed a fine sense about what was and what was not productive activity; they felt resentful and betrayed. The librarian in Hayward, who had devoted endless hours to the development of the labor market information system, complained: "We're being systematically destroyed."

There was no time for job search interviews or workshops. That marvelous piece of hardware, the occupational data bank, became idle.

The imposition of ESARS was followed in February 1972 by an edict from the regional office of the Department of Labor: "The name of the game is placements. Increase the placement count."

The effect was to place all other activities in disrepute. The three project offices were left out on a limb. The full force of the bureaucracy discredited the experiments and turned in the opposite direction. With no source of agency approval and no hope for reward, there was no way for the managers to continue the experiment on their own. Although the hardware and some of the physical aspects remained, the activities had to end.

In March 1972 the consulting team engaged by the Department of Labor began an evaluation of the Hayward project by comparing the three experimental offices with three control offices.

Although the evaluators recognized that the project was no longer viable and had been distorted beyond recognition, they continued to use their measuring devices. They noted that one of the three control offices had already adopted a number of Hayward features, which meant that it had lost its value as a representative control office.

In December 1972 the evaluation report was published. It concluded that there were no measurable differences between the Hayward offices and the others.

The effect of such a report on the Hayward project was insignificant, since it had already ceased to be a viable experiment. Unfortunately, the report served to support those forces driving for a return to the straight labor exchange mission, those individuals who deplored change and experimentation. The report also stimulated the further retreat of whatever remained of COMO, and it had a deleterious effect nationally on any new attempts to develop and refine a usable labor market information system for the local office.

Nevertheless, the Hayward experiment had some impact on local offices. For quite some time after Hayward had abandoned many features of the experiment, the industrial and services office in San Francisco continued them. The manager attempted to get formal approval for counting workshops on the ESARS forms as "orientation." Approval was denied, and the workshops were discontinued.

Other features were discarded or fell into disuse as the burden of paper work increased. From July 1972 through November 1972 the industrial and services office accepted 3,667 applications. These were mostly the compulsory applications of food stamp recipients, welfare recipients, unemployment insurance claimants, and veterans. Since the job orders continued to be placed on the open market, this was all strictly paper work; it had no value to the staff or the applicants. In addition, during the same months, 7,514 ESARS I forms were completed. This meant two different forms were taken on each of 3,757 applicants.

Despite the seemingly overwhelming odds against the Hayward concepts, an office in Stockton, California, undertook extension and refinement of most aspects of the experiment. With the active assistance of the regional research unit, a revised and refined occupational data bank was introduced. Plans included audiovisual and other devices to better orient the public to the services in the office and to the use of the labor market information system. The office also developed a program directed toward employer involvement and participation of the larger community. In view of the agency direction, many of the staff members in Stockton had little hope for the success of their effort.

The lessons of the Hayward experiment are many, but perhaps they can be summarized by two important observations. The first is that there are substantial problems in the nation's multifaceted system for evaluating, training, and distributing its human resources. The problems are most acute with regard to those individuals who are locked in the so-called secondary labor market and who have little access to standard entry channels. They are manifested vividly and daily to those employment service workers who deal with those individuals on a person-to-person basis every day and who struggle constantly to resolve the conflict between what they know should be done on the front line and what they are told to do in some authoritarian directive.

The second important observation is that some part of the solutions to the problems must come from those same individuals on those first few front-line echelons who can intuitively assess the pragmatics of delivery systems. And some part of the solutions must also come from those same individuals who walk into employment service offices each day seeking help . . . and find frustration. The public acceptance of or hostility toward an agency posture *is* playing a part in finding solutions, if the vote is counted.

WHITHER THE
EMPLOYMENT SERVICE?

All viewpoints presented in earlier chapters are observations of one individual participant and are limited to one constricted geographical area. Since leaving the employment service and my own counter point some four years ago, I have participated in a number of national studies which allowed me to observe the procedures, examine the data, and interview staff members in more than 25 offices throughout the country. The similarities of problems and attitudes in all parts of the nation have reinforced many of my own conclusions and perceptions, have broadened some of them, and have altered others.

The assumption that the northern California agency had gone further in restructuring itself to serve the disadvantaged was clearly confirmed. Employment service offices were affected in a variety of ways by the events of the 1960s. Some went through the changes in form and rhetoric only, with little change in content — and they openly admit this. Others remained totally unaffected and are even now replicas of the 1962 office described earlier. One office, a COMO office, suffered from the onslaughts of ESARS and changing emphases from the Department of Labor, just as did the Hayward office. Still, the COMO office did have a great orientation toward gathering and giving information to job seekers and it presented a good atmosphere for clients.

The advent of the Job Banks program strongly affected the outlook of all the offices where it was installed, because they relinquished the specialized occupational desks in favor of centralized order taking. The resistance to any change at all was expressed in one office by refusal to allow the public to examine the jobs. In that case the office simply replaced the old job order boxes with Job Bank viewers, which were available only to the interviewers. Apparently, nothing would move that particular system to "open up."

This type of schizophrenia was evident everywhere; there were two souls in one body.

Some important differences did exist among offices which provided new knowledge and which added insights to some of the problems which have been discussed earlier. One of the studies in which I was involved was an effort to evaluate the effectiveness of institutional manpower training in meeting employers' needs in skills shortage occupations.[1] Employment service offices were important to the study because the selection of occupations for MDTA training is based on the occupational knowledge of the employment service and on the transactions which take place within the employment service structure in a given labor market. The study took research teams into fourteen cities, where they examined three subsystems within the employment service — the research and statistics units, the MDTA system, and local office transactions. Research methods included interviews with staff members and examination of the two computerized information systems, ESARS and Job Banks.

It seemed logical to assume that the system itself would have analyzed its own data, charted its own labor market, and identified skill shortages. It also seemed logical to assume that in the process of installing two computerized systems a method would have been developed for interpreting the printouts and staff members would have been assigned and trained to analyze the information so that it could be of value to local administrators, manpower planners,

[1] Olympus Research Corporation, "Evaluation of the Effectiveness of Institutional Manpower Training in Meeting Employers' Needs in Skills Shortage Occupations," Salt Lake City, Utah, 1972; summarized in Garth L. Mangum and John Walsh, *A Decade of Manpower Development and Training,* Olympus Publishing Co., Salt Lake City, Utah, 1973.

and evaluators. Both assumptions proved to be wrong. If these capacities existed, they were well hidden.

There was no usable system for identifying skill shortages, and no evidence was found in any of the fourteen cities that a methodology had been created for interpreting computerized data by anyone for any purpose.

The ESARS counts all local office activities, including placements. Job order takers carefully feed into the system *all* information about each job opening they receive. But nothing comes out of the system that tells anything about those orders. Interviewers carefully record and feed into the system every action taken for a job seeker. But nothing comes out that tells how useful those actions were to a job seeker, if at all. The main purpose of ESARS is to provide state and federal governments with a budgetary and evaluative tool with regard to the local office. But it does not really describe anything. If a counselee finished a session by physically assaulting the counselor, ESARS would still record it as a "service to the applicant." It gives nothing to the local office interviewers or the job seekers; it provides nothing new by way of a local managerial tool; it offers no labor market information out of all those orders; it gives no increased capability to determine exactly what the local office is doing in its particular labor market.

From discussions with 22 different managers, only one was found who had the slightest notion about how the ESARS printouts could possibly help him. ESARS reports were universally deplored and despised. What ESARS does give the local office is a headache, a shower of paper work, and a sense of absolute conformity. There is simply less time to help anyone. And good programs have been felled by the deluge of ESARS paper and ESARS definitions. If a local office had any ambition to develop a decent occupational library for its public, or if the office had a notion that a disadvantaged person would gain by learning something about how to be interviewed, ESARS would provide the final discouragement because there is no way to be credited for such activity on the ESARS forms. It provides the exquisite stamp of absolute sameness in every office.

In a 1971 report entitled "Falling Down on the Job," the Lawyers Committee for Civil Rights Under Law and the National Urban Coalition attacked the employment service in a scathing fashion for its failure to function on behalf of the disadvantaged. And yet, the same document applauded ESARS, cautiously, as a "clear-cut opportunity for stronger and more effective federal direction of the state agencies." If the central motive is to "control" the employment service, the position is understandable. But if the objective is better service to the disadvantaged, then ESARS and the poor are in direct and open conflict. In terms of how staff members must divide their time and focus, ESARS and the poor stand at opposite ends of the spectrum. Of course, it is possible that potentially valuable information may be produced by ESARS. But it matters little if no one knows it or uses it.

It appeared to the research teams that the research units attached to the state agencies were in most cases nothing more than outreach arms of the Bureau of Labor Statistics in the Department of Labor. They had little relationship to the selection of MDTA courses and even less relationship to the development of local labor market information. They were not required to use either their skills or their data to provide a staff service for local manpower administrators or planners or — what is even more important — to local interviewers and job seekers. Given the entire apparatus, including the research and statistics unit, a person looking for work in any city still could not get solid information in an employment service office about entry routes into an occupation in that town. It seems an anomaly for the research units to be attached to the state employment services. If not a service to *that* line staff, in *that* agency, why be there at all? Why not simply be what they are — branch offices of the Bureau of Labor Statistics?

The contrast of most of the fourteen state research units observed with the direction taken by the northern California research group was stunning, further evidence of the spinoff effect that resulted from the extraordinary efforts in that area during the 1960s, when field staff requested and expected help from the research unit — and they got it.

The analyses of the Job Bank printouts were most revealing, and the findings relate directly to the central question of employment service mission. For the purposes of the MDTA skill shortages study, it was necessary to obtain the most refined and detailed information available about the occupations in which employment service transactions took place in that city. What kind of jobs did employment service offices deal with? Did this flow of job orders provide the employment service with the necessary data to gain insight into the range of occupations existing in the broader market? Was the knowledge residing in the agency front-line staff, in its research staff, or in the computer sufficient to determine a skill shortage appropriate for MDTA training?

Just as with ESARS, the elaborate Job Bank installation had not been programmed to clarify or synthesize any occupational information. It was almost as if both systems had been deliberately programmed and planned to prevent anyone from identifying exactly what type of jobs the employment service dealt with. The Job Bank tables listed job openings and placement activities by two- or three-digit codes from the *Dictionary of Occupational Titles,* without job titles. Because of the structure of the third edition of the Dictionary, this broad grouping in no way defined the exact occupation or the level of skill. Thus "good" jobs and "poor" jobs could not be distinguished. One could distinguish between professional, technical, managerial, clerical, sales, service jobs, miscellaneous work, and so on, but that told nothing. An apartment house manager's job for a couple with no pay carried a managerial code. Good paying, highly skilled jobs in transportation were coded in the miscellaneous category. A computer operator or a full-charge bookkeeper both took a clerical code — and so did a two-week job as a file clerk. Sales occupations included highly paid industrial salesmen who make $25,000 a year as well as straight commission salesmen selling door to door. Each of the structural, benchwork machine trades and processing groups included low- and high-skilled jobs. For an interviewer who had written the order and knew just what kind of jobs he was handling, the Job Bank printouts were models of obscurity.

Of the many tables and arrays of data produced by Job Bank, only one printout listed jobs by the more detailed six-digit occupational codes, without titles. It was called "Report on Unfilled Job Openings," and it reported openings, placements made, and orders unfilled for thirty days or more during the month. The tables were available on a monthly basis, but states had the option to reject that report, and many chose to do so. In actual fact, it made very little difference since no one did anything with the reports. In many cases, state officials did not even know that they received these tables. The national office stored most of the other ESARS printouts for each state but deposited this one in the waste-basket. It did seem that the entire employment service operation had a stake in not coming to grips with exactly what occupations and jobs it dealt with. Reports could be obtained for only seven of the fourteen cities studied.

A simple frequency analysis of these tables proved to be overwhelming in its implications. For example, in one city during April and October of 1971, 54.8 percent of the total placements were in two occupations — casual labor and phone book delivery-man. In another, three occupations — warehouseman, materials handler, and domestic day worker — accounted for 55.4 percent of the placements. (Some cities included domestic workers and casual laborers in their Job Bank printouts; some did not.) In a third city, 43.1 percent of the placements were for materials hand-lers, construction laborers, factory helpers, landscape laborers, and warehousemen. And so it went — with some variations — from city to city, always showing an extraordinary concentration of activity, both openings and placements, in the lowest skill, least stable, lowest wage secondary labor market. There is little doubt that there would be variations in different labor markets, but it is a safe assumption that the function of the employment service in those seven cities reflects the national picture. In fact, both com-puterized systems contain the potential for detailed analysis of exactly what the employment service does and a profile of its relationship to the outside labor market. It is not the absence of data that prevents self-examination. One suspects that it is rather an absence of policy.

From these findings, a series of questions and conjectures arise: Why is the Pandora's box kept closed? Why does the em-ployment service appear to have so little capability or interest in looking at what it actually does in the labor market, whom it serves, and whom it does not serve? Who are the employers that need and use the public employment service? Is it, indeed, func-tioning primarily for the purpose of supplying a labor pool to the employers who pay low wages and operate with nonunionized employees? And if this is so, is this a valid social function for the manpower arm of government?

That the job transactions were concentrated at the lower ranges of the job market is not particularly a new finding, although it is a confirming one. What is most significant in the study of Job Bank printouts is the limited way that the computer was used and what this says about the concept of mission that permeates the agency. In city after city there actually was an unexpectedly *wide* range of occupations represented in job order transactions that *do* pass through the system. The data indicate that they pass through infrequently, but they do pass through. Even though there was an overwhelming concentration on a few limited occupations, it remains a fact that there were 639 different occupations represented in the job orders in one month in one city, 441 in another, 358 in another. The orders come and go, and they constitute a small proportion of the gross transactions, but the valuable information about an occupation that is contained on the job order is irretrievably lost. Every order yields more information about who hires in that occupation, what skills and knowledge are required on the local scene, whether it is unionized, what hours people work, the wage range, what training is required, and a myriad of other job-related details. If the computer — instead of the interviewer's brain — had been asked to capture, accumulate, sort, store, and recapture such information . . . over a period of time it would be extensive. It would provide a respectable body of knowledge about a wide spectrum of occupations in a particular labor market. It would provide a data base for the interviewer. The Job Bank computer, because it was not conceived as a labor market information tool, was not asked to serve this function.

There is a widespread assumption that local office staffs absorb (by osmosis, perhaps) a large body of information about occupations in local markets because they receive job orders from employers, interview applicants, and visit employers occasionally. When a research team approaches a city and asks about occupational information in that city, both research and administrative staffs always direct the team to the local office. They are "the people who know." From sheer exposure, it is assumed that the local office staff knows which occupations are in short supply and if they are appropriate for institutional training programs. It is assumed that staff members can deal knowledgeably with an employer about his occupational needs and that they are expert enough to provide job seekers, educators, and manpower planners with solid knowledge. For this assumption to be correct, certain conditions or alternatives would have to prevail:

(1) The office would have to operate with specialists on occupational desks.

(2) The transactions in a single occupation would have to be extensive and frequent enough to provide a full picture of all the variables and complexities within a particular occupation.

(3) This would have to be true over a wide range of occupations.

(4) In the absence of occupational desks, the information would have to be centralized or exchanged so that it could be stored, retrieved, and used by all the staff.

The analysis of the Job Bank printouts and the interviews with the local office staff established that none of these conditions prevailed. Before the advent of Job Bank, a placement interviewer assigned for five years to deal with a particular occupation could have accumulated a respectable body of refined local information about that occupation. Even then, however, there were many problems connected in that source of information. The interviewer carried it in his head, and the information left with him when he was transferred or became ill. Often the information was narrow and limited to a particular segment of the total market which had been "cornered" by the local office — the tunnel vision syndrome. However, most offices are no longer operating on the basis of occupational divisions of work, and there is no person who "knows best" — if there ever really was one. An order for an air conditioning mechanic may be taken by one person one day and by someone else a week later. A rod and chainman coming into the office may be interviewed by one interviewer and placed by another five days later.

The advent of the Job Bank and centralized order taking reduced the possibility of the "osmosis" process. It is more difficult now to find the one person who knows most about an occupation. The sad thing is that the Job Bank, with all the costs it entailed, with with all the bits and pieces of information flowing through the system, did not provide a replacement or an improvement for that lost expertise, however limited it may have been. This is precisely what the occupational data bank in Hayward attempted to do, no matter how crude and pioneering the effort.

In summary, although Job Bank does provide the local public with microfilm viewers for Job Bank books so the job seeker can scan the listed openings, it does not add a single new job to the generally dismal array. In northern California, the jobs were opened to the public with far cheaper teletypes and cellophane wrappers. But for the rest of the nation, where jobs were hidden in little boxes, it *is* a positive step. Yet, despite the expensive equipment, the interviewer is no better equipped to respond to the inquiry of a job seeker who wants to know what companies hire people with his skills, no more knowledgeable in talking with employers, and no more prepared to deal with manpower planners. In terms of the local office needs, the Job Bank only serves to display the jobs. Potentially, it could have served a far more valuable purpose.

This thesis takes on even more validity when it is viewed from the vantage point of serving the disadvantaged. No single group in the community has a greater need for information about the wide range of occupations than the disadvantaged. After listening to men in the ghetto discuss their occupational aspirations and job search activities for three years, the staff in the Adult Opportunity Center office could recall no more than thirty occupations that were ever the subject of discussion.

There is a continuous demand on the employment service to do what it cannot do, what it is powerless to do. In the case of computer use it *was* within the power of the agency to provide a broader service and a better tool. That power was not used. Administrators and planners have little inclination to plan a service for that population which walks out without a job referral, because unless a "transaction" occurs there is no official acknowledgment that such a population even exists. The labor exchange myth dominates the planning function.

The absence of adequate local labor market information as a local office tool is clear and unmistakable. But whether it is the absence of data that creates the most significant problem in selecting occupations for manpower training for the disadvantaged is a dubious assumption, although heard often. The charge is frequently made that the employment service does not develop training programs with job potential because it had inadequate information. "Falling Down on the Job" makes that charge from its position of advocacy for the poor.

An interesting bit of history bearing directly on this problem came to light in the course of the skills shortage survey. When MDTA was passed in 1962, it was intended mainly for those who were being displaced because of technological reasons. The big concern of that period was the revolution in manpower needs that was anticipated from the development of the computer, and MDTA was intended to retrain those displaced. At that time, the federal MDTA handbook was written. One chapter — chapter two — spelled out for the field manpower planners a rather complicated and sophisticated system for studying the marketplace, making projections to determine its future needs, and developing training programs in relation to those needs. The search was for occupations that would be in such short supply as to ensure "reasonable expectations of employment." But in 1964 policy changes began to occur. Black demand was powerful and MDTA goals were shifted from the technologically displaced to the disadvantaged. Congressional committees called for a more relaxed view of "reasonable expectations of employment," and directives of that nature went to the field. Training programs were for the disadvantaged. It was clearly no longer necessary to establish a skills shortage or rigid criteria for selecting occupations or trainees.

Chapter two of the handbook was not rescinded; it fell into disuse, as is so often the case in any bureaucracy that responds to political and social pressures. Manpower training administrators filled out all the MDTA forms and said the right words, but no one was very serious about establishing that an occupation be in genuine demand at the time or would likely be in demand in the future. It is not that the field workers failed to do what was expected. Quite the contrary. They got the loud, clear message and did precisely what was expected of them by Congress, by the agency's own officials, and by the political leadership. The message was: "Open the training programs to quiet the raging ghetto, and do not hold with the 'Bible' on how you do it."

To use MDTA for helping the disadvantaged to become somewhat more competitive for any valid job — or as a form of subsistence — is *not* the same thing as using it to answer the shortage needs of employers — either current or projected. The same vehicle cannot do both, no matter how it is squeezed. Realistically, chapter two of the handbook was obsolete, inoperative . . . only nobody said so. It does seem odd, now, to be critical of the employment service for its failure to serve the disadvantaged, and at the same time attack it for not adhering to more rigid methodology for selecting training occupations.

The projection of manpower needs, even as a general activity, is valid and necessary for many purposes, including the whole education field, but it is not an exact science. Neither the economy nor political decisions that affect manpower needs are so orderly and predictable. Even when projections are accurate, they may not be heeded by more powerful forces and considerations. The market often corrects its own imbalances long before any effective governmental action can take place. Witness the cycle of engineering projections since World War II with employment service, school, and veterans counselors periodically discouraging or encouraging training for engineering according to the latest projections, usually wrong. On the other hand, projections accurately warned about an oversupply of teachers, but this was of little avail against the bureaucratic tendencies of colleges and universities to maintain and even increase their teacher training programs.

There are innumerable additional factors that influence the choice of occupations for training other than projected shortages, a few of which should be mentioned:

(1) The Department of Labor and the state agencies do not have the power to force industry to share its plans with government. Industry considers that its plans for expansion, redirection, technological change, and location change are its own business. Hence, data usually deal with the past, not the future.

(2) Employers themselves have little knowledge of their future markets, do very little real planning, and thus could not accurately project future manpower needs even if they were willing to do so.

(3) A six- to nine-month institutional training program for

an unskilled, unlearned person cannot develop a skill level high enough to be considered in short supply.

(4) The restraints in MDTA against training apprenticeable occupations, the restraints against academic training, the opposition of unions . . . all further reduce the possibilities of relating training programs to the needs of the labor market.

Because of these factors the employment service tended to select occupations for training programs that were large, had a high turnover rate, required some skill component, and were not already staked out by other job-matching mechanisms. This is why so many of the courses throughout the country were for welders, auto mechanics, clerk typists, and health occupations. These are large occupations with much turnover, and even if the occupation was declining, it still presented a better chance for work and a better risk for training than occupations which may have been growing but were very small or required years of training. In the year 1969, fourteen selected cities developed 69 training programs in new occupations that did not fall into the customary array. None survived more than a year for a variety of reasons, not the least of which was that it was (and is) more possible to get a newly trained welder or a service station mechanic or a beginner clerk typist *some* kind of job than to break through doors not so easily opened for the new, lightly trained diesel electrician or refrigeration mechanic. It was also true that educational facilities were not prepared to teach new courses. And of course, the whole matter of selecting trainees for programs mainly by poverty criteria created a mix that literally precluded statistical success.

These, then, are the serious and realistic problems that have bedeviled the employment service and lie at the root of the narrow occupational choices under MDTA. It is such considerations that contributed to the limited success of MDTA. These are of far greater significance than the inadequacy of the agency or the absence of labor market information for planning purposes. Knowledge of the market would help — it might make things easier for MDTA planners to a limited degree — but it would not *significantly* increase or widen the occupational choices available to MDTA planners. In some intuitive way, the field workers know this. People grinding out MDTA programs sensed that a great effort spent on extensive labor market studies would not actually give them much more elbow room in occupational selection for MDTA — given its own limitations, the limitations of the marketplace, and the limited range for selection of trainees. Where the collection, storing, retrieving and interpreting of local labor market information would in fact make a huge difference is in the local offices. It is there that the information is needed every day.

The Labor Exchange: A Viable Mission?

More basic than failure to use all available information to further the employment service role in manpower training are issues related to the enabling legislation itself, the 1933 legislation that generated the agency and defined its universality of mission, the Wagner-Peyser Act. Because that act established that the employment service installations were to act as job-matching brokers everywhere in the land, the Department of Labor has based all of its operations on that single purpose, that single function, and thus it has produced a single evaluative device for every installation in the country, whatever other vagaries and embellishments have appeared at various times.

This is where it all seems to fall apart, like a house of cards. This is what the ESARS monstrosity reflects. This is why every office looks alike, acts alike, and shows so little capacity to respond to its own realities. The whole system overlooks the fact that there is *not* one labor market. There are many markets, and they may all have quite different potentials for the job-matching function; quite different kinds of activities might be indicated to facilitate the operation of the market in different locations. Even within the same city, different groups of occupations have vastly different needs for a public employment service — and far different placement potential.

In some communities, particularly small ones, the economy is stable and somewhat stagnant. There may be few alternate job-matching mechanisms and no large disadvantaged population. The labor market exchange model suits that marketplace very well. The employment service plays a valid traditional labor exchange role and fulfills a need for both employer and job seeker. The office may have considerable weight in such a community. But this is a rare situation in our complex society. In most cases, the labor exchange model is a gross misfit for the modern labor marketplace.

In no place is the misfit so clearly and dramatically seen as in Alaska, with its sparsely populated, broad expanses, its severe weather conditions, its unstable, itinerant work force, its strong union control of hiring mechanisms, its absence of industry, and its traumatized native population in transition between cultures. Alaska's wage and salaried employment averaged 92,400 in 1970. Of this total, 35,600 were employed by government. On a yearly average, 6,900 were employed in contract construction. Alaskan labor is heavily unionized. Two industries, government employment and contract construction, represent 46 percent of all the jobs, compared to 22 percent nationally.

Generally, the employment service would consider government employment and contract construction as a fair proxy for *zero* placement because of union hiring and civil service systems. In Alaska, the civil service systems are less formidable obstacles to employment service involvement than in other parts of the United States because of the instability of the work force in Alaska. Temporary state jobs *are* placed with the employment service and offer a limited placement potential, especially in Juneau, the state capital. However, one wonders about the labor exchange value of an employment service in the Nome area, for example, where 60 percent of the work force is in government jobs. A posting of jobs on the local drugstore bulletin board might serve the labor exchange function just as well. Yet, Alaska has droves of job seekers from the "lower 48" in the early summer, who flood the employment service seeking jobs, information, and advice.

The absurdity of a single-mission concept is most clearly seen in the bush areas. In Alaska there are ten one-man manpower centers located in remote communities. Two of them, Kotzebue and Barrow, are located inside the Arctic Circle in native Eskimo villages. The centers there were actually established to extend the expected jobs from the North Slope Prudhoe Bay oil development to the natives, but that has not emerged.

Three-quarters of Kotzebue's population of 1,875 are Eskimo. The city is something of a tourist attraction and serves as the center for polar bear trophy hunting. There are no more than two hundred jobs in all of Kotzebue. The manpower center manager, a young native Alaskan who had been in the agency some seven months, was discouraged and depressed when the research team visited him in 1972. In his seven-month tenure the office had processed 99 application cards. Four individuals had been counseled, two had been enrolled in training, and 31 had been placed on jobs. The jobs were of a temporary, casual nature.

The biggest employers in Kotzebue are the native hospital, employing sixty or seventy persons, and the Bureau of Indian Affairs. Unemployment is variously estimated at 70 to 90 percent, depending on how one chooses to interpret the cash and subsistence existence of most of the Eskimos. Snowmobiles have replaced the dog teams. No young Eskimo in his right mind and with access to an occasional television advertisement would spend hours fashioning an *ulu* from bone and slate when the local store sells an aluminum knife for $3.00. But hunting and fishing for subsistence provides neither the $3.00 nor the gasoline for the snowmobile. The trauma of transition is palpable.

The young manpower center manager was troubled because he did not really know what to do. He had been told that his goal was "placements," and he had been trained for three weeks in the Fairbanks office in the use of manuals, forms, ESARS, and reporting methods. But there were few jobs, few applicants who came in (many who did were town drunks known by all of the six employers in Kotzebue), and the jobs were all short term and low pay. Kotzebue had no vocational counseling service in the community of any kind. There was one social worker associated with public health, and the Bureau of Indian Affairs had a school counselor in the high school, but neither of those individuals had any vocational orientation. Since the center manager was not a counselor, he did not feel that he could deal with the myriad needs and problems that were rife among those who came into the office. He had been informed when he came on the job that the employment service had got rid of the previous manager because he "had failed to do his job, had become involved in all kinds of native affairs, and did not send his ESARS and other forms in on time."

Barrow is the oldest and largest native village in Alaska. It is located deep into the Arctic Circle, at the northernmost point of land on the continental United States. It is also the closest sizable community to the Prudhoe Bay oil development. Barrow is a famous old commercial whaling port, and the Eskimos there still engage in whaling for subsistence.

Of the 2,300 inhabitants of Barrow in 1972, three hundred were white. There were between 250 and 300 jobs, 100 of which were with the Naval Artic Laboratory, an installation for scientists from all over the world. The community had no piped water and no sewer system. Tourist accommodations were primitive, to say the least. Barrow had no high school. The cost of living was so high in the village that a quonset hut rented for $400 a month.

The community resembled the classic colonial picture. The three hundred whites lived on the federal installations with running water and bathing facilities. They had their food and beverages brought in from Fairbanks at government "Post Exchange" prices, which made it unnecessary for them to confront the village prices of $1.50 for a dozen eggs. Those high prices were reserved for the natives, who had an unemployment rate of 70 percent and a wage rate of $2.50 an hour — when they could find employment. Welfare and subsistence hunting and fishing sustained the native population.

The manpower center manager in Barrow was a native Alaskan who was deeply involved with native organizations and activities. His comments reflected the more sophisticated native thinking in the manpower field. The contracts and commitments for pipeline work being negotiated at that time threatened to preclude involvement for the Barrow Eskimos, and he feared a repeat of past experiences in the Ketchikan and Sitka pulp mills where the new industries did not mean any gains for the natives.

Of course, the manager had been given brief training in forms, manuals, and ESARS. He knew that his purpose was supposed to be placements and passivity — matching men and jobs in the office. But he eschewed that role, and in his position as native leader he played the advocate of the people. When the Naval Arctic Laboratory maintenance camp work was subcontracted to a new company in October 1971, the manager immediately solicited work for the local natives. The company maintained that it could not recruit through the manpower center because of union contracts. Threatening to take compliance action, the manager was able to write an MDTA provision on this job-training contract, using funds granted to the Alaska Federation of Natives, with the approval of that organization. The commissioner of human rights in Alaska had proposed a "cluster hire" program whereby two Alaska natives would be hired for one job alternately, with time off for subsistence hunting and fishing. To the manpower center manager, this appeared a valid way to ease the Eskimo into the cash economy. He had begun to press for this concept in dealing with subcontractors at Prudhoe Bay. All of these dealings were conducted from his position as vice president of the Alaska Native Association; none were performed from his position as employment service manpower center manager. His training, the goals of his agency, and the ESARS forms he sent in did *not* validate any of this activity. The only validated activity over an eight-month period was the registration of 245 persons, of whom 14 were counseled, 11 were enrolled in training, and 54 were placed in jobs.

There sat two manpower centers in the desolate Arctic, in the half light of the 24-hour sun in May. Children wandered the streets at four in the morning because there was no place to go; their parents were drunk. There — when the Arctic Ocean, the sky, and the tundra mixed into one grey-whiteness — sat an office with a counter, a tiny replica of a New York City office. These offices had it all — the blank application cards, the ESARS forms, the blank job orders, the desk, and the telephone. And facing the public was the counter. What the office did not have was a single piece of information about what the world was like away from Barrow or Kotzebue, or how people earned their living in those distance places — not a word about occupations, nothing to take to the high school or junior high school to intrigue or stimulate youngsters with any idea of what they should learn or how they would earn. But there was ESARS. And ESARS had no place on the form to check for *that* kind of activity.

Despite national office directives and ESARS, it is possible to conclude that Barrow *is* different from New York City and that the two are more different than they are alike. Somehow a national manpower policy should make it possible to acknowledge that difference.

The inappropriateness of a single-mission concept for the entire nation may no longer matter. The competency or focus of the agency may not be a significant factor in determining its viability as a labor exchange. The options may no longer exist, and decisions taken by the agency as to its direction may be of little consequence. Whether in Barrow or New York, the agency seems to be intrinsically impotent. It is peripheral to the heart of the job market and can neither control nor significantly influence any of the elements involved in the availability or distribution of jobs. The job market may already be carved up; all the claims may already be staked out; and all the deals may already be consummated. It appears as if the preempted employment service has no claim to partnership — it simply is not where the job exchange action is. It is hemmed in, with little elbow room. Yet, it is still in the center of the job search action. It is still used by the public looking for work, if not by the employers seeking employees.

If this is true, if the employment service has in fact been preempted, then no amount of exhortation to staff to make more placements will alter this. Nor is it possible to blame employer "disenchantment" on the emphasis of the 1960s on service to the disadvantaged. Was the employer ever enchanted? Is the enabling legislation and the rationale that broght it into being — the Wagner-Peyser Act — still relevant in its present form? Is it still viable, still reflective of a social and economic need? Has it become obsolete? Or does it perhaps require strengthening and revision in order to ensure a more open, central market for jobs?

Since the passage in 1933 of the Wagner-Peyser Act, which established the labor exchange role of the public employment service, there has been an immense proliferation of competing job-matching mechanisms and systems. These mechanisms now have a huge vested interest in maintaining themselves. The union hiring hall — in fact, the labor movement generally — has become a major job-matching operation since 1933. Government employment — city, state, and federal — has grown to such a point that it incorporates a huge segment of the work force which is controlled by rigid civil service recruitment and hiring systems. The large personnel offices in most major business concerns retain the application cards of throngs of job seekers and perform all the recruiting, selecting, and hiring processes for the firms. All vocational schools — which have vastly multiplied with technological changes since 1933 — perform placement services for their graduates. Professional and trade associations engage in placement services. All colleges and high schools provide a labor exchange service.

Private employment agencies, particularly in the clerical and technical fields, have mushroomed. Temporary employment agencies which act as labor contractors are comparatively new, but they are growing and have completely captured the temporary clerical job market. (This last example is an obvious instance where the employment service, because of its rigidity, ineptitude, and sluggishness, failed to fill a vacuum which existed.) Newspaper help-wanted ads perform an open market labor exchange role which may, in fact, be nearly as successful as that of the employment service and which involves many similar kinds of jobs.

It matters little whether these mechanisms have developed because the agency failed to fill the need, or whether there were other, independent reasons. The hypothesis is that these various entities have taken over the broker role to such a degree and in such a large portion of the primary labor market that, under normal conditions, the employment service is left with little *placement potential* other than the low-pay, unorganized, low-skill, high-turnover secondary market.

This is a hypothesis that can be tested with research. Private firms do it all the time. They study their market potential, including their competition, before they establish their operation. It would be disastrous to an industrial enterprise if it pretended that the competition did not exist. And yet, the concept of examining the placement potential of a given market in relation to its built-in competition is foreign to the employment service. The recent decision of the Department of Labor to redirect itself toward the labor exchange role was arrived at without a glance at whether it is a "possible" program, whether it can be accomplished, whether it is needed, or what the cost will be.

If the hypothesis is true, then the historic and persistent loss of job orders and placement have little to do with whether the employment service is "good" or "bad" or *where* it decides to put its energies. If there is little placement potential, the best agency in the world could not successfully lure the employer away from his established source for manpower. There is a way that it could, but only if it offered him even more careful screening, even more exclusivity. Shall the employment service now say to the employer (as the Department of Labor appears to be saying): "We have erred in our emphasis on the disadvantaged. We shall sin no more. And if you place your orders with us, we will ensure that you will no longer be troubled with the minorities." Is this the essence of what is being said to the staff now, despite the rhetoric in other directions? Most systems can select their clients. Under Wagner-Peyser, the employment service presumably cannot. It has to take all comers. It could surreptitiously drop the applications of most of its clients into the wastebasket and concentrate its efforts on vying for the employers' business by working only for the favored few. But this is hardly a noteworthy social activity, especially if the alternate placement mechanisms are working satisfactorily.

However, if it were determined that the institutions and systems that do operate in the marketplace are functioning in a fashion that is too exclusionary, too discriminatory — too punitive, costly, and exploitive to a large segment of the work force when it becomes unemployed — then something more is needed, legislatively and administratively, than the mandate provided by the Wagner-Peyser Act, which merely establishes the labor exchange function and assumes its voluntary use by employers and public.

There is another great difference between 1973 and 1933. In that forty-year period there has been an immense change in consciousness about the role government must play, whom it is obliged to serve, and when it has an obligation to intervene, order, and control. For government to unabashedly take its position on the side of industry against the worker or the public was accepted as natural in 1933. When workers went on strike, there was little rationalization or rhetoric necessary to justify the use of militia and the force of government power against the worker and in open service to employers. Although Wagner-Peyser and other New Deal legislation began to move government toward a greater commitment to the welfare of the people, it was just the beginning of the process. The great liberal innovations of that era may now be lagging behind the newer consciousness of social needs. It may be lagging well behind governments of other countries in the role they play in the manpower field.

In "Falling Down on the Job" the recommendation is made for a phased compulsory listing with the employment service of job openings in all public service jobs, all jobs at all levels of governments, all jobs with private contract employers, and all jobs occurring with employers involved in interstate commerce. The report suggests the possibility of *exclusive* compulsory listings for a specified period of time.

These proposals are no panacea, and there are many serious concerns about the consequences. Under Executive Order 11958 requiring government contractors to list openings with the employment service in order to give preference to Vietnam war veterans, employers often list openings because they are forced to but with no intention of hiring anyone referred. This results in a good deal of paper shuffling, useless trips by applicants, and an inordinately high rate of cancellations. But it has brought a wider range of job openings into some of the local offices.

However imperfect a solution, the proposal touches on a basic problem related to the mission of the employment service, because it recognizes the fact that mere manipulation of the supply is not effective and that there is a need to make an incursion on the demand side of the marketplace. The fact is that without increasing access to the jobs when they become vacant, the employment service is helpless. What is more, a considerable body of job seekers not attached to a closed job-matching system continues the haphazard milling about in search for work. The recommendation implies that all manpower programs and all delivery systems are addressing themselves to a marketplace that is now controlled solely by the employers, without restraints and without accountability to the general social welfare.

The field of ecology offers a fairly good analogy for such an incursion and a good example of change in consciousness since 1933. There is now an awareness that society as a whole must intrude upon the right of industry to destroy the air, the forests, the rivers, and seas, and that it must do so to protect its collective existence. In consumer affairs, too, the change in consciousness about the government's role is becoming evident. Inroads are being made or attempted through consumer action and through legislation to intrude upon the unrestrained *caveat emptor* philosophy of an enterprise. In consumer affairs, as well, the sovereignty of the marketplace is being challenged, questioned, and sometimes curtailed.

Compulsory disclosure of job openings to a public market could be regarded similarly. The serious question to be determined is whether that sovereignty, that exclusive right of industry to control jobs has failed to provide satisfactory answers for large numbers of people, and whether that failure thereby jeopardizes the social good even more than compulsion. It is ironic that a public employment office exists and yet not even state, federal, and local government agencies regard their own creation any differently than they do a newspaper, an individual, or a private agency to whom they mail their civil service listings. Even government does not use the public employment service. The employment service appears in the ludicrous role of standing, hat in hand, hoping — and often pleading — that *somebody* uses it. Aside from all other considerations, it is a discomfiting image, lacking in dignity and of dubious social value.

The costs for administering public employment offices come from a portion of the unemployment insurance payroll taxes. Essentially, the employers are paying the bill. This raises some intriguing speculation. If the large employers have so little use for the service — as the evidence clearly indicates — if the service does not play a significant role in filling their manpower needs, why have they appeared to be so silent and uncomplaining? Is it possible that the employment service fills a need for the business community other than as a source of manpower?

After reading the 1973 Manpower Report to the President, a writer observed in the *Wall Street Journal* that the Department of Labor spelled out publicly, "with unusual candor," that it was redirecting its policy and telling all state agencies that "rebuilding responsiveness to employer needs is a key objective in all major labor market areas."[2] The lead sentence of the article was: "The employer is back in the driver's seat at the U. S. Employment Service." The loss of placements, attributed to the orientation toward the disadvantaged during the previous decade, was offered as an explanation for the policy shift. Is the "redirection" founded on careful analysis or is it another hasty shift in policy, based only on hope that a viable role will emerge? It is time to ask the deeper

---

[2] Calame, Byron E., "U. S. Employment Service Switching Focus from Minorities to Supplying Skilled Labor," *Wall Street Journal*, March 12, 1973, p. 14.

questions and to seek a more profound analysis than that which is now permeating the field.

The Employment Service and the Disadvantaged — All Fall Down

The dichotomy which has permeated manpower circles in the past decade can be characterized as a pull between two points: Point A — the labor exchange orientation — has been dealt with in preceding chapters. Point B — the orientation toward the disadvantaged — is best articulated by the study, "Falling Down on the Job," published in 1971 by the National Urban Coalition and the Lawyers Committee for Civil Rights Under Law. Prepared by advocates for the poor who were examining the employment service from the outside, the study found that the policy toward the disadvantaged "was never really embraced or implemented by tradition-minded state officials who remained strongly oriented toward employers' needs." Attacking the employment service as a 38-year-old moribund bureaucracy, the study accused it of frustrating the goals of federal manpower programs. It charged the agency with responsibility for failing to meet the manpower needs of the disadvantaged and asserted that the capabilities and goals of the employment service were in direct conflict with the needs of the poor.

The study's main inventive contribution to helping resolve conflicting needs is the proposal for two separate agencies — one for the poor and one for the "job ready." The agency for the poor would assess, orient, counsel, and provide intensive individualized service. (The reader will perhaps forgive the deep, weary sigh that such a proposal would evoke in a San Franciscan. It sounds so very familiar. We've been there before, and we did not just visit, we stayed all night. In no way does this path ensure better solutions for the disadvantaged. The same proposal comes from those who want to rid themselves of the albatross of the disadvantaged so as to forge ahead as a respectable labor exchange. Northern California ran the gamut on two separate functions. In no way did it ensure greater acceptance by the employers or better service to the disadvantaged. These are obsolete solutions that deal superficially with the problem.)

Because "Falling Down on the Job" was not constrained by government controls and because it commanded national publicity, it is regrettable that the opportunity to move the dialogue forward was missed. The entire position is rooted in the assumption that the employment service does, indeed, have the power, the control, and the resources to do the job assigned to it. It is implied that it failed because it is a poor agency with bad attitudes. Whether or not the charges made by the report are true, the really great crime committed by the employment service is *not* that it failed to "meet the manpower needs of the chronically unemployed," as charged. The crime lies, instead, in accepting the mission as if it were feasible, in deceiving itself and everyone else about its capacity to solve problems it cannot even influence, let alone control.

All these years the employment service has stood before Congress asserting its capacity to take on any offered mission, just as it now asserts that it can place welfare clients on jobs or get them off welfare, just as it now insists that it can get back in good with the employers and become a vital labor exchange agency. There has never been anyone to say, "No, it is not possible, not for us or for anyone else without the tools or the teeth to carry it out." The crime lies in not forcing redefinitions and in not raising public awareness of a need for valid solutions. It lies in allowing the employment service to be used as a buffer, a sandbagged wall between the enormity of social need and the paucity of social response. It lies in a public agency functioning to maintain itself rather than to alert the nation. In the buffer role, it has helped obscure from the national awareness that the economic and political power of the country has *never* committed itself to instituting the profound, organic changes without which the efforts of the 1960s are studies in futility.

"Falling Down on the Job" falls into the same trap. It also accepts the mission as being feasible. It is a good, safe report. It directs its guns on the buffer and, by and large, continues to engage in the same inconsequential mock battle.

The history of manpower efforts in the last decade, with their unprecedented focus on the disadvantaged running head on into the cynical fiscal manipulations designed to increase unemployment, makes it crystal clear that the primary question and the only valid question left must be *what* is being delivered and not the delivery system. Whether it is or is not the mission of the agency, or which agency is to be used, or what minor rearrangements can be made about how to group agencies and how to send people through elaborate tracking systems are peripheral if not obsolete issues. We have simply come to the end of the road, that detour which bypasses the main question and leads nowhere. Worrying and quarreling about what color the tires should be is absurd when there is no motor.

The parallels with the published disclosures of the decision-making process in the Vietnam war are unavoidable. The final insanity — an undeclared war, committing over half a million men, a country nearly destroyed in order to "save" it and spare our leaders humiliation — can be traced back, step by step, to one false axiom based on self-deception. Each level, each segment was locked into previous assumptions and previous commitments, creating the apparent necessity for the next step. The germinal questions were not asked, the basic assumptions were never challenged until they were lost in antiquity. That is exactly how the manpower field has operated. Neither the Department of Labor in its currently policy switch nor "Falling Down on the Job" are questioning the basic premises. All each is really saying is that if you deploy your troops a little differently, you will win the war. Neither asks if it is the right war, the right enemy, or the right troops.

Evident throughout the language of legislation and manpower documents is a formulation, a construction that goes to the heart of the problem and reveals the turning point in the thinking. Repeatedly, the literature talks about how the agency is expected to "meet the manpower needs of the disadvantaged." And then the writer proceeds to believe his own rhetoric. *Agencies* in themselves do not meet manpower needs. The manpower needs of the disadvantaged — or for that matter, the skilled worker — are met when the agency has access to an abundance of decent, permanent jobs. The needs are met when the agency can offer extensive, relevant training which leads to jobs. The needs are met when there are cheap and adequate child-care centers near where a woman lives or where she works, when transportation facilities are available from the central cities to the outlying job sites, when jobs pay enough to warrant going to work and getting off welfare. Any agency with that kind of power and resources will meet the manpower needs of the disadvantaged. *No* agency without them can do anything but toy with the issue, go on its own "trips," build its own empire, hand out little nibbly tidbits, keep alive a special lexicon of words as if the magic words constitute genuine manpower services and answer a need, play authoritarian, self-servicing, counseling, "case carrying" games, and lull itself into thinking that a referral of somebody once a month to vocational rehabilitation is something meaningful called "supportive services." Or it can invent a new agency to play the same game with variations — the proposal offered by "Falling Down on the Job."

In 1970, ten different interviewers working in various poverty area offices of the employment service in San Francisco were quizzed about the relationship between the resources and the people they interviewed. They were asked to estimate what percentage of the people they interviewed could be fitted into *any* of the resources available to them, including jobs, all training programs, and accessible supportive services. Their estimates ranged between 5 and 10 percent. What would be done for the other 90 percent in a new agency? Down there at the front lines it is of little consequence under whose aegis those encounters are taking place. When the interviewer sits with the client, his mind is rifling through all the cubbyholes for solutions, for a way to end the interview with something real, something specific to offer, to give, or to say. If the cupboard is bare 90 percent of the time, it would matter little from which agency the interviewer got his paycheck. It is not the *agency* that fills that cupboard or keeps it bare. It only dispenses what is there. The sources of power must be addressed, not its servants — which are government agencies. Only at the various seats of power and wealth, where fiscal and economic policies are set for the country, can the decision be made to uproot those conditions which make and breed the "disadvantaged." Either those in power will make the decisions or the people will make them, but the agency can't.

One can engage in a dreamy, idle reverie. Suppose — just suppose — there really were bulk programs, commensurate with the need. Suppose there really were enough jobs — good jobs — and training programs for everyone, as there were in World War II? Would there be very much concern about who or what delivered that service? Would there be this much emphasis on personal problems, on "rapport" and pseudopsychiatry? Would not the interviewer with knowledge about jobs, industries, and companies be more valuable to the client than someone who was the same color or talked sympathetically to him in Spanish but had no job knowledge or experience?

It is hard to escape the conclusion that most manpower programs and most concepts of delivery systems spring from unexpressed and unacknowledged mental sets. One is that the basic fault or failure lies not on the absence of opportunities, but on the part of the jobless. Another is a profound unrecognized and unexpressed acknowledgment that there is very little real substance being offered; other mechanisms and activities are substituted to obscure that knowledge — ignore and intimidate, or smile the professional smile, or diagnose and "treat."

A Personal Plea

My own experiences during the past twenty years have convinced me that the tug of war between the two points in the dichotomy is no longer valid. The dialogue is being conducted at a superficial level because neither position deals with the deeper questions and problems. The debate is obsolete, locked into an unproductive, circular jousting match from which can come no resolutions, no rethinking, and no further insight. It has been exhausted. It has run its full course. What is needed is a new dialogue, a redefinition of the problems with more depth, more knowledge, and more sophistication. Both sides are dealing with peripheral issues. Neither represents genuine options.

I do not feel that I have enough knowledge to fully define the perimeters of a new dialogue or to make the necessary theoretical analysis. It would betray the whole intent of this book if I were to offer my version of solutions or blue prints. I have none. The internal logic of this exposition would lead me to suggest, tentatively, that there are two ends to the spectrum of possiblities: Either the Wagner-Peyser Act is no longer valid and the employment service has outlived its usefulness as a facilitator of labor market activities, or the job market must become more public, more ordered, and more accessible through government intervention, with the employment service as the vehicle through which this is accomplished.

I do not believe that there is enough objective knowledge now about how the market operates or what role the employment service plays to arrive at a definitive conclusion. What is more serious, I do not believe such knowledge will be sought and obtained unless the deeper questions are asked. They are not being posed now. It is time to surface and confront exactly for whom the employment service operates, who it does and does not serve, and whom it should serve and with what. It is time to recognize the absurdity of a single-mission concept, a single method of delivery, and a single criterion of effectiveness for every one of the myriad installations in the country.

My own personal prejudice, stemming from the years of dealing directly with the job seeker, is that a public marketplace for jobs must exist, but it must be far more open and accessible than it is now. That job seekers should pay exhorbitant fees for getting a job is just as distasteful to me now as it was to the framers of the Wagner-Peyser Act. That job seekers should spend time and money following the will-o'-the-wisp, inadequate information provided by a newspaper want ad or word of mouth constitutes, in my eyes, a social wrong and is most punitive to those who are not already within the job system. The value to the economy of the employment service in preventing unnecessary loss of wages or worker productivity because job and worker must go in search of one another was one of the arguments for establishing the employment service in 1933. Whether this is still an important factor, however, is a question for economists to answer. The current reality, no matter what the original intent, seems clear. The mere existence of a public employment office has in no way ensured its use.

It is hard to imagine a national manpower policy that ignores the unemployment and underemployment levels in the ghettos. I am not knowledgeable enough to define that point in the policy process that would produce genuine answers, either in terms of jobs or through some form of guaranteed income. But if manpower programs are directed to the ghetto, they must no longer suffer from gross inadequacy. So far, they have reflected shallow, dated misconceptions about how the labor market functions, arbitrary and mechanical concepts about the nature and cause of the disadvantaged state, and faulty, untested axioms about behavior-changing techniques. Though they confer benefits to a number of individuals, they are basically predicated on the premise that the goals can be met by manipulating the supply, without power to affect and intrude on the demand, without altering and interferring with the basic economic policies and priorities of the country. In my eyes, however, there is no longer any doubt that the emphasis on the social worker's intensive, individualized service approach, unaccompanied by genuine solutions, is inappropriate, diversionary, and unbalanced. It helps to create and sustain myths for the job seeker, for the staff, and for the country.

Whatever its goal or its mission, it is no longer acceptable that this agency or any other should serve itself instead of the people. However weak its power, it has no moral right to worsen the situation for the user. It has no right to run him around, to make the search for work even more depressing and disheartening through its arrogance. It has no right to intimidate or withhold anything from any users anywhere, most especially not from the poor and the black. It has no right to promise, explicitly or implicitly, to do something it cannot do.

The dividing bureaucratic counter, with all of its broad implications, is no longer tolerable. It must be transcended.

AFTERWORD

by GARTH L. MANGUM

This is an angry book and an important one. But the anger is not at the public employment service. There, the emotion is tenderness and sympathy toward an agency in which the author has spent most of her career. She knows the yearnings to "do good," the masking of feelings behind bureaucratic brusqueness to steel against the frustrations of impotence. She views an agency and a staff committed to improving the lot of all unemployed and underemployed people, but trapped by a system which requires them to act dishonestly because the system is basically dishonest about the realistic role of the institution.

The federal-state employment service bears the scars of innumerable attacks over the years. It has been "damned if it did and damned if it didn't." To fill the employers' demands was to "cream" the crop of job applicants and neglect the welfare of those who were competitively disadvantaged in the labor market. To seek to serve the disadvantaged was to alienate employers and deny equal access to job orders by all job seekers. New assignments and new programs have constantly rocked the agency, and new priorities have been established without relieving the agency of responsibility for the old ones. And all of that has been perpetrated by policy makers outside the system.

All of this has been said before. But Ms. Johnson's book is unique in several ways. It is unique for me because it examines the role of the employment service from the inside looking out — from behind the counter — rather than as an outside observer looking in as has been done by Adams and Bakke and Hoaber and Kruger and Mangum any many other academics. But the authenticity of her inside vantage point is not her most important contribution. It is her open declaration of the inevitable and ineradicable impotence of any agency submerged in a system beyond its control, yet forced to justify its existence by claiming a virility it can never attain — not only the impotence that exists but the misleading promise that precedes it.

Ms. Johnson does not place blame on the agency but on the policy makers outside it who assign it its role. She does not regard the basic dishonesty and impotence as being beyond redemption. Not eunuchry but assignment to an unfulfillable role is the enemy of virility. There is, she says, a valid and fulfilling potential role.

The issue is which form of public intervention into labor markets can improve their functioning for all participants, especially those least able to meet their own needs? Matching workers and jobs can be achieved only if there are "handles" to both. Placing workers in jobs implies some control over (1) jobs and (2) employer recruitment selection and hiring practices. The employment service can have the latter only in time of labor shortage or in the unlikely event employers are forbidden to hire without its intervention.

But since employers need workers and workers need jobs, factors which keep desirable matches from occurring are:

(1) An excess or shortage of workers or jobs

(2) Workers lacking the characteristics required by employers

(3) Jobs unattractive to workers

(4) Workers or employers lacking knowledge and access to each other

None of these factors are surprising. The appropriate question is which of the factors fall realistically within reach of public employment service influence. The employment service cannot appreciably affect the numbers of workers and jobs. It has no control over the processes by which attributes and skills are acquired by most people. Even with the manpower training programs inaugurated within the past decade, the number of training "slots" available can serve no more than the barest margins of those needing help; limited resources have dictated entry-level preparation for only rudimentary skills, and these skills are useful only where jobs exist. Where the worker characteristics which are unattractive to employers represent prejudice rather than objective judgments of productivity, the agency is powerless. Nor can it change the nature of employers' jobs.

To Miriam Johnson the sin of the employment service lies not so much in its weakness vis-a-vis labor market influence. Her charge is against failure to face those weaknesses honestly as facts of life. It is the effort to create a facade of potency by attempting to monopolize what it does not own which annoys the author of this book. She objects to the efforts expended by the employment service in justifying its existence statistically by recording numbers of transactions rather than providing openly what it has to give.

The most obvious departure of the real world from the economist's model of the competitive labor market is in respect to the availability of information. The need for more effective labor market information systems is a current cliche in the manpower business. But it is something more complex that Ms. Johnson is advocating. The labor market information systems called for by most writers would once again be under the monopoly control of the bureaucrat; it would be information provided by the employment service to the manpower planner in order to allow him to manage the workers' (and employers') labor market welfare for them. Ms. Johnson's notion is a simple and achievable one: (1) make easily accessible all possible information about where to search for whatever jobs exist, and (2) teach job seekers how to effectively search for employment.

These are not entirely new, original, and unique suggestions. Her experience was with the Hayward office, but a few other employment service offices are open and attractive and counterless, or display job orders in the lobby for preview by "self help" customers. For example, only a few blocks from where I write the new Salt Lake City office of the Utah State Employment Service is friendly and inviting, designed for the comfort of the job applicant rather than the convenience of the bureaucrat. It has no counter; it reaches out, in a sense, to bring in and embrace the walk-in customer. Job orders are on open display. Friendly assistance is available for filling out applications. A statewide computer system can search all job orders to match them with applicant skills or all applications to match them with employers' needs. But even this advanced example does not go far enough. Even such operations maintain the appearance of job monitoring by only describing the job; they still require the applicant to approach the officialdom for a referral to find where a job is — whether or not that officialdom is barricaded behind a counter.

But Ms. Johnson goes further than asking for open access to job orders. She sees value in using all possible information — old job orders and applications, computerized Job Bank, and other data — to identify employers who hire in desired occupations, regardless of whether they have current openings. Train employment service staff members to become experts in the structure of community labor markets and in techniques of job search, she asks. Let them inform labor force members of alternative sources of training, of new ways to acquire skills, and of the availability of supportive services. Forget defensive recordings of transactions performed. Become the lubricant in an improved labor market machinery.

Remarkably, the recommendations are neither expensive nor exclusive of present employment service activities. Nor are they difficult to achieve. In fact, they accord with what little is known in job market theory. To achieve the recommended changes requires mostly modesty, giving up the myth of job monopoly, some retraining of staff, analysis and display of available information and gathering of more, and above all honesty as to what can be delivered. It should be tried.

However, these recommendations are more profound than they appear, challenging the very existence of a public employment service in its present form. They aver that the world has changed and suggest that one of the sacred landmarks of social legislation may be obsolete. Many vocational educators suffered when they saw the Smith-Hughes Act of 1917 give way before a new philosophy in the Vocational Education Act of 1963. The original premise had been that education was irrelevant to the employment of all but a few, and that the role of vocational education was to meet the limited skill needs of the labor market. By 1963 it was obvious that preparation was becoming vital to most citizens, and the policy concern was to be the employment needs of people.

Perhaps where Smith-Hughes promised too little, Wagner-Peyser promised too much. More than anything else, the New Deal marked the legislative recognition of the insecurities in the labor markets of an industrial economy. By that time most individuals had become dependent upon wages and salaries in the fluctuating economy; they were no longer self-employed or in subsistence agriculture. And there were no information sources, no labor market intervenors to aid employee and employer in facilitating their groping toward each other.

But the labor markets of the 1970s have intervenors galore. Union hiring halls, federal, state, and local civil service commissions, company personnel departments, private employment agencies, temporary employment services, professional and trade associations, schools placing their own graduates . . . all compete in the arena which the public employment service had almost to itself in 1933. Under such conditions, the long-term decline in employment service placements may not be cause for alarm. It is built into the structure of the labor markets, although aggressive effort may increase the "market share" of the employment service.

One possible interpretation of this conclusion might be a call to eliminate the public employment service. The private fee-charging agencies have been advocating that for some time. An embarrassing question seldom asked is: What if there were no public employment service? What difference would it make? Interestingly, only in the area of manpower services to the disadvantaged (now to be subsumed into a larger concentration on placement in general) is there clear evidence that something happened which would not have occurred in the agency's absence. It is to be supposed that the agency's general presence does make a difference, but there is no evidence. No one knows what a cost-benefit analysis of the total employment service operation would show.

The Wagner-Peyser Act does, in fact, specify that the labor exchange function is the primary function of the employment service. According to the act, the U. S. Employment Service was to:

. . . promote and develop a national system of employment offices for men, women, and juniors who are legally qualified to engage in gainful occupations, including employment counseling and placement services for handicapped persons, to maintain a veterans' service to be devoted to securing employment for veterans, to maintain a farm placement service, to maintain a public employment service for the District of Columbia, and, in the manner hereinafter provided, to assist in establishing and maintaining systems of public employment offices in the several states and political subdivisions thereof in which there shall be located a veterans' employment service. The bureau shall also assist in coordinating the public employment offices throughout the country and in increasing their usefulness by developing and prescribing minimum standards of efficiency, assisting them in meeting problems peculiar to their localities, promoting uniformity in their administrative and statistical procedure, furnishing and publishing information as to opportunities for employment and other information of value in the operation of the system for clearing labor between the several states.[1]

Over the years, lawmakers and administrators have found no difficulty in adding to the functions of the employment service. Could they legally subtract from them?

Miriam Johnson's final passionate plea for dialogue would suggest to me discussion not of abolition of the public employment service but of a radically different role, one which would encompass the operational changes already enumerated but go far beyond them. In effect the changes would call for a reversal of present and historical emphasis. Where the employment service has been first a labor exchange with other aspects of labor market intervention appended according to need and circumstances, it would become a general agency for labor market interventions, supplying only what was not otherwise available, including the labor exchange functions.

As Ms. Johnson notes, one of the constant surprises to anyone dealing with employment service personnel is how little general knowledge of the local labor market exists in the various

---

[1] 48 Stat. L. 113, June 6, 1933, as quoted in William Haber and Daniel H. Kruger, *The Role of the United States Employment Service in a Changing Economy*, The W. E. Upjohn Institute for Employment Research, Kalamazoo, Mich., 1964, pp. 26-27.

offices. If the employment service is to cease its uniformity in Barrow and New York City, if it is to be honest about its impotence in job control and move toward its potential strengths, its first requirement will be for more knowledge and more analytical skill in assessing the needs of each local labor market. Such capabilities are vital, even in those labor markets where the priority need is for the traditional labor exchange. But these are probably a minority. More often workers need a listing of employers who employ workers with their skills, plus instruction in job search techniques. Employers will be well served as they are more knowledgeably approached. In smaller communities, employment service offices are already looked to for guidance in economic development — a viable role, given enough analytical knowledge.

It is notable that with the development of the Cooperative Area Manpower Planning System (CAMPS) and manpower revenue sharing, the employment service has been viewed as a potential deliverer of manpower services but rarely as an important resource in manpower planning. That role would seem natural, and its failure to materialize points up the surprising lack of labor market knowledge in most local offices. In part it may be a result of the lack of any meaningful manpower planning. The issue in most CAMPS and with the emerging manpower planning councils has not been planning, in a meaningful sense; it has been who is going to have what control over the distribution of federal dollars. Meaningful manpower planning must occur at the labor market level, and it must identify problems, set objectives, examine and choose among alternatives, monitor and evaluate programs . . . all of the components of a classic planning system. It must lead from problems to solutions, and they will be different for every market. Is there a role there for employment service personnel? Manpower skills training does, in fact, require the dual role now supplied by the employment service to identify persons needing training and occupations with skill needs. But at present the assignment is too often met by placing whoever is unemployed in available slots in whatever training programs seem to have had a reasonable placement rate last time around — usually a high turnover occupation.

This, then, is the vital message of *Counter Point*. The counter has not only been a barrier to serving the needs of job applicants, but it may have made an anachronism out of the whole notion of a public labor exchange, no matter how attractive such a notion may be. Is it possible to design and operate an agency sufficiently flexible to supply whatever intervention is needed by each specific labor market? Can there be bureaucrats *that* open minded and staffs *that* knowledgeable? If not that challenging role, what is left for the public employment service? And if that is indeed the role the public agency should fill, is the present agency appropriately structured to fill it?

At any rate, both academics and practitioners of the manpower arts should be grateful for one who has bridged both worlds and coupled hardheaded practical experience with objective analytical insights. Manpower policy and practices cannot but be enhanced. The employment service is making a concerted national drive for revitalization. The time is appropriate to respond to Ms. Johnson's appeal for dialogue.

INDEX

191